MILLIONAIRE MANNERS

The Men's
(and Boy's)
Guide to Social Grace in the New Age

WRITTEN BY
SADIQ ALI

BRINKTANK PUBLISHING
Baltimore, Md, USA

PUBLISHED BY BRINKTANK LLC

Copyright © 2014 by Sadiq Ali

Cataloging-in-Publication Data is on file with the Library of Congress

Library of Congress Control Number:

ISBN: 978-0-9960644-0-8 (paperback)

Visuals Designed by: Jerrold Daniels, Daniels Design Group

For more information write to us at Brinktank LLC,
P.O. Box 47033, Windsor Mill, MD 21244 or visit us online.

SPECIAL SALES

Brinktank Books are available at special discounts for bulk purchases for
sales promotions or premiums. Special editions, including personalized
covers, excerpts of existing books, and corporate imprints, can be created
in large quantities for special needs. For more information, write to:
info@Millionaire-Manners.com

For more information visit us at:
www.Millionaire-Manners.com

15 14 13 12 11 10 9 8 7 6 5 4 3 2 1

PRINTED IN THE UNITED STATES OF AMERICA

Dedication

To my Father.

I strive to make you prouder.

Table of Contents

Part Three: MANNERS

EPILOGUE:

PART ONE:
ATTITUDE

CHAPTER 1

An Introduction to Etiquette. From etiquette basics of seven-year-old grace to Millionaire Manners.

Manners and Morality Go Together Like Peanut Butter and Jelly.

We hear the word manners, or the word etiquette and it elicits different reactions from different people. There are those who think this "manners stuff" is a complete waste of time. Others think it could work for them, but they've never really been in a situation which required knowledge of such things. And still there are some men (and young men) who have been confused, mystified, befuddled and outright confused on what they should do in certain settings and have been waiting for this guide. I have written this book for all of you. I just hope and pray it makes it into the hands of the folks who need it most!

Etiquette in the most simple of terms is knowing what to do and when, while offending the fewest number of people and impressing the most. Therein lies the very delicate balancing act that is attempting to please everyone in every situation. If you are looking for that answer from within the pages of this book, keep looking. It doesn't exist, and he who is looking for that magic pill should plan on dedicating many, many years (his whole life) to such a cause. One of the first lessons on etiquette and manners is to first realize, that no matter what you may do in certain situations, you will offend someone. However, one of my primary objectives is to arm my readers with as much ammo as possible to come out of the everyday awkward situations looking unfazed. If you take to heart the lessons presented here, and practice them in earnest, you will be a changed man (or young man), and be offered all the spoils that come with this.

In this book you will also learn how manners and etiquette should never be just a show, or veneer behind which it is acceptable to lie, cheat or steal just because you are polite about it. To people looking for this type of hustle, the information in this book will not work for you because you do not have the proper intention in your heart and mind. The intention should be to become a better person, period. I will say that some of the techniques presented here are so powerful that even if utilized by the unscrupulous or disingenuous, they will work, but only in the short-term. I hope your objective is not to look for short-term gain, but rather to change how you behave fundamentally. You will succeed in the long-term, and gain more credibility, status and genuine friends than you ever thought possible.

Lastly, the habits you will have the opportunity to form during and after you finish this book will lay the foundation for success in whatever your endeavors are, and assist with whomever you wish to become. When in doubt, just think back to all the lessons of being a gentleman that your mother or grandmother tried teaching you growing up, and you will have at least some familiarity with half the material in this book. But there's a catch: Grandma didn't grow up with the Internet, social networks, cyber bullying or Match.com, nor the complexities that present themselves living in the 21st t century.

Think of Millionaire Manners as Grandma's lessons updated for the new millennium. She would be proud!

What is the definition of Etiquette?

We defined etiquette firstly as knowing the right things to do at the right time, while offending the fewest number of people. This is a great definition to get you started, but an advanced definition could be knowing the right thing to do at the right time, while making yourself feel the best about you. This is a mouthful I know, but sometimes what separates those who have class is sometimes as simple as how they feel about themselves, and not the way you feel about them, that radiates from these individuals and makes you envy them. Having you feel great about yourself is another chief aim of this book. We live in a society full of people, organizations, etc. that attribute great value to things that really deserve none. What is more valuable than most anything is ultimately how you feel about yourself, and what value you place on growing your own self-respect. Many of the terrible things that people do to one another stem from having no value for their own lives, and having almost zero self-respect. Many psychologists have written and studied extensively on the subject of self-respect and love being the most important ingredient in anyone's quest to love another. Again, at the root of this project is giving the reader the ammo to love themselves, radiate true happiness, and watch everything else fall into place.

This book is also about simply being human. Sometimes we look to vague words, descriptions and job titles to define or categorize who we are. Before you are any color, race, nationality, religion, or any other association, you are first human. The human family is the largest in the world and you didn't have to do anything to become a member other than be born! Knowing this fact should make you feel very good. After you read this book you will become an ambassador for human rights across the globe, because the cool thing is that everything we talk about in this book is completely transferable across international borders, different races, tribes etc. Meaning, one of the last definitions for etiquette could be learning to function at the highest level of humanity and learning to become an ambassador for human rights wherever you are. Lofty objectives I know, but trust me, we will get there.

Why should you care about etiquette?

As you're beginning to read this book, you've probably already thought at least once or twice, who cares about being polite? That's a good question. I'm also sure you've already thought getting good at this "manners stuff" is also going to be a lot of work, am I right? Be honest. No matter your answer, what I will tell you is that it is fun learning this information, and it's not that difficult to learn and master. Based on your instincts, you've probably been ignoring the right things to do for a while now. Part of what we will teach you is to do what your instincts tell you. If you have to ask whether something is proper in a given situation, then it probably isn't. This is one of the most basic litmus tests you can give yourself right now. If you'd like to experiment even further and before you get into the meat of the book, try asking yourself what your gut tells you to do in certain situations, then do it, and watch a completely different result happen than what you are used to.

Bottom line is that having proper etiquette, knowing proper etiquette, and actually using this etiquette will immediately set you apart in any setting. This book breaks down exactly how it will set you apart in detail. Places like the classroom for our younger readers, your workplace (and I do mean any workplace), your place of worship, dates, job interviews, social settings and much more. Our world is moving faster today than it ever has before, and tomorrow it will be even faster, so anyone who takes the time to actually say please and thank you, and do the five seconds extra worth of these items leaves a lasting impression you would be shocked at. In a sea of silver fish, does it hurt to be remembered as the one fish that day that was purple? I promise you it doesn't. Showing extra respect and treating everyone like a somebody is also deeply rooted again, in how you feel about yourself. There's an old saying: "hurt people, hurt people," that I want you to keep in mind while reading this material. It means that until a person is healed or satisfied with themselves, they can never outwardly project goodwill and cheer.

How proper etiquette can get you friends and keep friends.

In his seminal classic, *How to Win Friends and Influence People* (upon which many of the principles in this very book are based), Dale Carnegie tells us that you can "catch more bees with honey than vinegar." As we talked about earlier, with so many people going out of their way to be rude on a daily basis, imagine the impact on everyone around you when you go out your way to be the exact opposite. Positivity is like reverse field radiation, and instead of repelling everyone and sending them running away from you because you can get sick and die from radiation, positivity has the reverse effect. People will naturally and consistently be drawn to you and your nurturing light and aura. This is because people do not gravitate toward negativity, they gravitate toward positivity. The more positive you are in your daily interactions, the more productive and fulfilling relationships you will have.

People we consider friends want to be encouraged and feel better after a conversation with us or after they leave our presence, not worse. By engaging in good etiquette and using Millionaire Manners you will actually be sought out for your kind words and thoughts because people will come to know you as providing this. Friendship is akin to building a structure, where the more bricks you add to the people in your circle, the better. Same in the converse; the more bricks you take away from a person, via idle talk, negativity, angry emotional advice, et cetera, the worse off your friends will be. To show you value your friends is to show you value yourself, and in turn they will do the same for you. The name of this process is called edification, after the word edifice, which is another word for a building. Therefore the more you edify, or build up, those around you, the more they will do the same for you. The more positive energy you have radiating from your circle of friends and associates, the more insulated you can be from the harsh and negative world on the outside. Think of it as armor against negativity. The stronger your armor is, the more you can withstand on the road to your ultimate mission, which is becoming the best you possible.

Why is this book called Millionaire Manners when all millionaires don't have great manners?

Another question I'm sure you've probably asked yourself since you picked up the book, and (hopefully) purchased it, is why is it called Millionaire Manners, when not all millionaires have great manners? I would say to you, that is an excellent question! In another one of my favorite books, *How Rich People Think,* author Steve Siebold talks about a little known difference in the way people think, especially between the middle class and the world-class. The point is that he discusses how there are plenty of millionaires with a middle class thought process, and plenty of middle class folk with a world-class thought process, which usually means they are on the way to something much better. Therefore, Millionaire Manners isn't about showing off how smart you are, how polished you are, or pretending to be something you're not. Rather this book is about you being the best person you can be in every situation, not being intimidated by people who have more materially than you have, and most importantly helping you shift your mindset from that of lower, middle, and even upper class, to that of a world-class thinker.

The world-class thinker is immediately set apart in both thought process and action, and is always destined to have more, whereas a person with a different thought process who may have been blessed with some abundance today, is a very short play away from losing it all, and having no idea how to get it back. This book is only one of the first steps toward becoming a world-class thinker, an abundant thinker and thought leader among your circle of influence. Having people in the world treat each other better cannot possibly be bad for this world we live in, and you can help make this a reality by using the principles in this book to be an example and model for this movement.

My first etiquette teacher was my father.

As you envision yourself shortly as a role model for all those you come in contact with for what it means to be civil, polite and downright respectable, first flashback to your earliest memories of what it meant to be polite. What do you remember your mother and father telling you? Do you remember what they told you? These are all questions for you to reflect on as you form your own etiquette identity.

I clearly remember my first etiquette teacher. That teacher was my father. Because my father was self-employed and also very active in the local community both socially and religiously, I feel I got a much more unobstructed view of my dad in action than most may have been privy to. I saw him deal with all sorts of people on many different levels. He served on the boards of nonprofits and also worked in his shops alongside his employees many hours per week. He was a managing member of our local house of prayer, and he even had his own radio show. He wrote for local newspapers and was asked to speak all the time. All the while I observed throughout these different inter-actions that my father maintained a level of consistency in how he dealt with people, and that standard was to treat each and every person well. He always led with a smile and a firm hand-shake. He also always began with a good word instead of revel-ing at the thought of being the bearer of bad news (which sadly some people enjoy). I always remember him telling me that you do a good deed not so someone can necessarily say thank you, but for you to feel good about yourself and so you that you can be square with The Creator. The Creator always pays all debts, so the more goodwill you float out into the atmosphere, the better off you will be. The point here is to remember that being polite is also a good deed.

You also want to keep in mind that on this point, as well as many others, conventional wisdom proves sound. That word is that in order to get respect you should give it first. This is another key element of demonstrating your Millionaire Manners, show-ing everyone you are giving respect as a *respectful* person, and therefore you should be given respect as a *respectable* person. They go hand in hand.

Why this subject should be taught in every school in America.

Child education experts all agree that the earlier you get cer-tain concepts into the minds of youth, the more permanently rooted they will be in their psyches. The good news is that we can teach our youth anything and have it leave a lasting impres-sion. The bad news is that we can teach our youth anything and have it leave a lasting impression! That is why this book is geared toward fathers and their sons, and that ideally they can read this book together. In the circumstances where this is not possible, I hope that every adult man that reads this book is already thinking of a young man whom they can either share this information with, or at bare minimum get them their own copy of this book. Doing this can potentially change our country. This is because the computer that is our subconscious mind can be taught to be self-centered and cynical, and to grow with the idea in mind that it's every man for themselves, and that the more ruthless I am, the further I will go. Or we can offer an alternative to this mindset, one where the subconscious is fed positivity, and that we strive to be the best versions of our current selves rather than contemplating how we can knock the next man down. Could some of this be why we aren't more civil and polite to one another? I believe so.

The shift in paradigm is crucial because although gender equality is on the rise, as it most certainly should be, men are still in the overwhelming majority of leadership positions throughout the country and the world. These are some of the same men currently in power who still think that the only way to solve the world's issues is through intimidation, war and espionage. I offer a different path, a path that says if we teach our young men early enough what it means to be civil, and to respect our fellow man, that these young men will grow into the leaders of tomorrow and may have enough forethought and subconscious armor built up so that they may try to solve the problems of the day with a slightly different approach in mind.

Frederick Douglass once said, "It's easier to build strong children than to repair broken men," and I firmly believe that. If we build the foundation of our youth strong enough, then our future will be that much brighter. However, if we expect things to be better through hoping and wishing, with no real change in our attitudes and in what we are teaching the generation succeeding us, well we might not have that much time left!

Etiquette could save you or your child from getting bullied.

I would like to offer yet another practical reason for reading this book through in its entirety. Bullying today is reaching epidemic levels. With the ubiquity of social media it happens faster and in a much harsher way than ever before. How can Millionaire Manners save you or your son from being bullied you ask? Great question. The answer here is also simple (sensing a theme yet?). Bullies prey on the weak, or should I say those they perceive are weak. However, it is usually not the case that the person being bullied is actually weak, just the bullied individual has failed to communicate to the world, and especially to would-be bullies that they are, in fact, not weak, and that bullies should look elsewhere for their kicks. This comes from etiquette. Knowing what to say, and when to say it is absolutely critical to success in any arena. We will teach you how to have the proper demeanor, one that says, "I'm not a tough guy, but I'm definitely no pushover." This book will teach you how the right posture and attitude can make you invisible to a bully before he even thinks of making you a target. This information will then allow for a quiet strength and confidence to radiate from your persona, actually making you a different person.

How can you use this book to change your life?

When a person truly wants to improve in something, all it takes is commitment to themselves for this to happen. No amount of desire attempted to be transferred from one to another can help if that individual does not truly want to be better. There is also one more ingredient here as well: Do you believe you can get better? Millionaire Manners is designed to ensure first you understand it takes commitment, but is also set up to help you develop the necessary belief to put it all together. Any time we tell our subconscious minds that we want to do something, it then runs a cross check against belief. If your computer comes back and says "ACTION CAN NOT BE PERFORMED," then you know right away your desires and beliefs did not match up. The good news is, you can change this pretty simply if you want. The first step remains commitment. Next is finding a teacher, or material broken down in bite-sized pieces small enough where you think you can master it. If you think you can you're there. As these two components work hand in hand, that is when the magic happens.

A bigger, better, badder self-image is what we are after. What is self-image? Well it's pretty much exactly what it sounds like. What is the image you have of yourself? Maxwell Maltz, who is one of the earliest users of the term, said this: "Self-image sets the boundaries of individual accomplishment." Maltz also came to believe that self-image was one of the "master keys," or the "golden key" to a better, more fulfilling life. If a person does not understand this concept, we might forever be fiddling around the "edges of the self," instead of its center. Positive thinking, for instance, might not be of any use if it is only related to our current set of life's external circumstances. Saying "I will get this job" will not do anything if the idea of being in the job is not consistent with how you see yourself deep down.

The more you work at this material, the bigger, badder and better your self-image will be!

The reasons why this is not a book to collect dust on your shelf

As the thoughts of this book presented themselves to me over the course of several years, I knew they would serve other people as much as they have served me over the years. I also knew that when it came time to present this information to others, I would vow to make sure that everyone who read this book would know that this book must be left off your bookshelf. This isn't a book to shelve after the first reading (or skimming). This is a book to be used day in and day out, until the material is part of your everyday behavior. When a carpenter goes to fix something he can only use what he has in his toolbox. If a broken door needs screws and he only has nails, that door is getting nails. What's worse yet is that some people don't even know screws exist! They only work with nails! No screws, glue, tacks, just nails. Having only nails is pretty limiting if you're that carpenter, so this book represents to the reader new screws, a screwdriver, glue and a glue gun. You must put it to good use and not think that having the nails alone will save you.

How many people do you know with horrible manners but don't know?

In psychology, there is a concept called the Jo-HarI Window. It speaks to the notion that each of us have four squares in our personality box. The first square represents things that you know about yourself and that everyone else knows too. The second square is for things that you know about yourself that no one else knows. The third square has things that you don't know about yourself but that everyone else has figured out about you. And you guessed it, square four is for those things you don't know about yourself and neither does anyone else. What in the world does the Jo-HarI Window have to do with Millionaire Manners? I'll tell you that there are some people who, unfortunately, have no idea how rude they are, and scarier still, have no idea why people avoid them. If you are one of these people, rejoice because in this very book we will discuss how to spot yourself going down a rude path, and also how to subtly correct and encourage those around you to behave in a slightly more polite manner.

Take a moment and think, how many manners, traits and personality characteristics do you have in each box? One of your personal objectives should be to have as few items in the last box as possible, with a secondary goal of knowing as much about yourself in different scenarios as possible. This is yet another instance of manners coming into play; knowing exactly what to do in each situation, and never becoming the person who has no idea he's offending everyone in the room.

One of the positive side effects of reading this book is that you will subconsciously become more perceptive of all the different interactions going on around you at all times; the grocery store clerk, the salesperson at the electronics store, the hostess at your favorite restaurant, the manager of same restaurant, and literally hundreds of more examples. Every day when you're out living life you should be paying attention to what worked in each of those exchanges and what, if anything, you would do differently if given the opportunity. Consider the conflicts you may have witnessed. Imagine, in each instance, how the offended person may have felt. . In most cases not happy at all. You now have an anecdotal reminder to not only make sure you never offend anyone in the same way (or at least dramatically reduce your offense ratio), but also to serve as a beacon for those who may be observing you, or having a bad day, on how to do things properly and like a gentleman, and more importantly, a human being.

What can be different tomorrow if you institute any of the concepts in this book?

If there's anything you can expect to be different tomorrow after reading this book, you can expect yourself to be different. You can never control the actions of others or guarantee an outcome even when you've done everything right. Stressing over this could drive you insane. But what you can do is significantly, and I mean significantly improve your odds at a great outcome by practicing what you read here and going out of your way to give the benefit of doubt to your fellow human being. People who don't stress about things they can't control tend to live longer, and live better as they do.

Picture also the possibility of making friends easier, receiving more love and adoration from family members, and bringing smiles to the faces of strangers daily, all because you have empathized with the recipient of a rude person's venom. You don't want to be that unpleasant person, especially with family members. Keeping excellent relations with one's family is a cornerstone of society that in recent times we have forgotten. And believe it or not, some family members you know and love don't invite certain members of the family around because of their manners. From a stranger's standpoint, here is a person you may or may not ever see again, but you've been given the ammunition to go out and potentially "pay it forward" from what you've shown them. Beautiful!

So as we begin, ask yourself, are you committed to learning this material and these lessons, and taking it to heart? Are you committed enough to not want to be "that guy" ever again-- you know, the one who damages relationships in his family, social circle and at work? Do you want to lead by example and watch doors open simply because you've made the conscious decision to be a better version of you? Do you truly seek to improve your self-image? Do you want to lead your children in becoming an ambassador for etiquette? A soldier for Millionaire Manners? If you answered yes to any of these questions, you are ready to embark upon a journey that will change you for the better, forever. Let's go!

Millionaire Morals:

- Etiquette is more than just manners.
- This isn't a manual to use to cheat with or use as a short-cut, but rather a tool with which to change yourself.

Action:

1. Write out your goals for reading this book.

CHAPTER 2

Why Millionaire Manners are the key to your life's Success (hint, it's attitude).

What is the halo effect?

We've already gone into some of the benefits to be realized from taking this information to heart. So here we begin to get more practical. As this information is integrated into your daily life, you will begin to be able to take advantage of what psychologists deem the "halo effect." A basic definition of this psychological phenomenon is the brain's positive bias toward an individual based on a singular trait or interaction that translates into their overall perception of this person. So what does this mean? It basically means that sometimes if you are nice enough to a person right from the beginning, they will have a hard time later attributing to or associating you with any negative characteristics. Pretty cool right? Again, this piece of information isn't meant to be used as a cheat, but rather it is yet another potential advantage and side effect of being nice and polite. Now if someone wants to promote you just because you say "good morning," everyday, that's on them. Just make sure you're ready for the promotion so they don't have to turn around and fire you too!

Because someone may rightfully over-attribute good qualities to you as a well-liked or successful person is no reason to take advantage of them. It is actually a prime time for you to prove this person absolutely correct and legitimately earn whatever accolades you may be receiving. Think of your Millionaire Manners as the gateway to your own substance, through which you need only be given time to fully let it shine through, then instantly become a winner. This book is not meant for shysters or tricksters, or anyone looking for cheap parlor tricks. Everything done with that spirit in mind will eventually backfire. This is about doing things the right way and *earning* your reputation as the gentleman you shall become.

What are the right habits to form?

Let's talk in a little more detail about exactly what your brain and subconscious will do with this information, whether you know it or not. We know from extensive studies that thoughts, beliefs and ideas lead to feelings and your state of mind, which lead us to actions and behaviors which ultimately lead to results. Picture it like this:

$T \rightarrow F \rightarrow A \rightarrow R$ = *Thoughts to Feelings to Actions to Results*

This simple formula should get your mind moving in the direction of thinking, that through these pages, we aim to change your brain, and give you new thoughts that will replace old ones, and replace mediocre feelings with those of focus and prosperity and change. These will get you moving and doing different things, good things, which will give you a brand new result. This should sound extremely exciting!

What we haven't gotten into so far is what happens when dedicated action is repeated with passion, consistently. This is called a habit, and it's what all winners have based their success upon. One of my other favorite definitions of habit is: *An acquired behavior pattern regularly followed until it has become almost involuntary.* Basically involuntary, auto-pilot, or unconscious! If you show me any successful person in the world, I will show you their collection of habits. Millionaire Manners will help you form many of these same habits.

The right habits help you form an overall positive mental attitude.

The belief and habits cycle also go hand in hand with your brand new positive mental attitude, without which, this information will not work. Some more good news is the fact that even if you are neutral or lukewarm about the information so far, you are still head and shoulders above the majority of society who think no self-improvement in the world can help them. They think they are doomed and wherever they are right now is as good as it gets. They see themselves as a victim in the cruel game of life, not knowing they control the outcome of the game. Unfortunately, these people are suffering from a negative mental attitude. In their world everything is bad, and is only getting worse.

However, as you build up your armor, and form your own positive mental attitude, you will slowly become impervious to the attacks on your mental real estate from these type of people. The sad thing is that many of them mean well. Others are just leaves in the wind and neither mean to help nor harm, and are just looking for someone to empathize and even sympathize with them and where they are in life. But when you develop your own positive mental attitude (PMA) the world becomes a much different place, one where you take responsibility for your destiny. It also allows you to become unflappable in the face of criticism and cynicism because you have come to realize and understand that most people are only criticizing and unknowingly tearing you down because they are too full of fear to be better at anything or at minimum, acknowledge they have anything to do with their own lives. As leaders we cannot allow ourselves or our loved ones to continue like this.

Great manners and etiquette will separate you in business.

We've gone into many of the benefits associated with becoming an expert and ambassador of this information. One area I cannot emphasize enough is how these rules will separate you in the business world. Hopefully you've heard the expression that "more deals are done on the beautiful golf courses of the world than in the boardrooms." If you haven't heard that before, there it is. But what does this mean? In the simplest of terms it means that relationships in the business world are everything. This means your reputation, your results and the perception surrounding you are critical elements to you becoming successful in any arena. Hopefully you've also heard b that people do business with three types of people; those they know, those they like, and those they trust. Wouldn't it then make all the sense in the world to master information and rules and form habits that can have you at least knock out two of three? If people can give you a halo within the first five minutes of meeting you, don't you think there's a good chance for them to want to get to know you, and eventually trust you too? Pretty low risk investment. In other words, the better you are at building relationships, real relationships, the better off in the world of business you will be. Just remember that folks are looking for something to bring a little bit of joy into their world. If you can do that by being your best self, you've already won half the battle.

🏵 Millionaire Mannerism:

You can only control two things in life; your attitude and your actions.

Great manners have their roots in spirituality.

One area we haven't touched on yet is where the roots of good manners come from. That's also an easy one. The world is filled with different religions and ways of life that give different rules and/or suggestions on how to worship The Creator, and ultimately how to live on this planet as smoothly as possible. Some of the earliest rules of etiquette I can remember come directly from the Ten Holiest Rules we know, also known as the Commandments. At least three of them, in my opinion, have a direct connection to etiquette and manners:

- Thou shalt not bear false witness against your neighbor.
- Thou shalt not covet thy neighbor's wife (or anything that belongs to your neighbor).
- Honor your mother and father.

These are just three of the universal laws we learned, not to mention not killing or stealing, etc. These are all based on spirituality, common courtesy, decency, and doing your part to keep the karmic scales balanced. Now whether or not you believe in karma is a topic for another book, but just remember that the universe never forgets, and usually, neither does a person whom you offend. While I've always said you should never do anything in this book because you expect something in return from someone, do understand that you cannot do good by other people for an extended period of time and not be rewarded. This is a universal law backed and insured by The Creator, and he always pays up!

Therefore, the notion of "Love thy Neighbor" isn't just for bumper stickers, but a tried and true philosophy that has immediate and profound implications in our present day lives. So you fulfilling this piece of the pie is moving us all toward a greater good, and a better society.

Making people happy around you through your actions will make you feel better about yourself.

Another one of the key benefits of acting better toward those around you, is that inevitably they begin to feel better, and so

should you! There is absolutely nothing wrong with this. Sometimes feeling good about yourself and what you've just done
is the best reward, and it begins to break the habit of looking
for someone on the outside to validate what you know is right.
Today we have plenty of people who will reverse validate bratty,
spoiled and obnoxious behavior many hundreds of times per
day via Internet and social networks. This is not any more right
than you looking for someone to pat you on the back when
something is done for the greater good. But even more importantly, you are training your mind, body and spirit on the art
of being selfless, and that is, again, committing an act solely for
the act itself with no regard or expectation of reward. Today,
among other things, we've lost the notion of what a selfless act
feels like, which has in turn caused us to largely lose the sense
of community that earlier generations enjoyed so much. But
when we regain it, it will be that much sweeter for the Millionaire Manners Ambassadors because then we can continue
to lead, teach, coach and train those around us in many different scenarios on exactly what this all means. The moral of
the story is to not expect anyone in the moment to understand
what your actions mean. Do them for the greater good and for
the example they set. Then when you do encounter someone
who truly understands and appreciates what you've done it'll
be all the sweeter. As the saying goes, "true happiness always
comes from within."

⚙ Millionaire Mannerism:

True happiness always starts from within, then flows
out.

Etiquette will make you make image conscious.

Another one of the main reasons for these lessons and information is to increase awareness and consciousness about the

everyday demeanors of those around you, and even yourself. It is impossible to study this material and make all the changes it calls for and not actively look for those changes in those around you. It's sort of like when you buy a new car, you suddenly notice every single one of the same type of car on the road when you're in yours. And it's not that everyone went and bought one at the same time as you, you are simply more *aware and conscious* of those cars now. It's the exact same thing with these principles: the more you study and use them, the easier you will spot them in others, and hopefully make the decisions to do more of what you see other practitioners doing, or less of what you see the uninitiated doing.

When you are able to master the perception portion of life, this is when you are truly able to see the types of strides you desire. The information in this book is dangerous because you are learning both style and substance, and therefore are able to change both what is going on in your mind, as well as partially control (or at least really play the odds) how people perceive you. As I have already stated several times, this is not a work of fiction that is full of theory and philosophical importance. All the principles here have been used by myself or other highly successful individuals in a variety of fields and professions. The common thread, however, is to first work on your insides, and then work on your outsides. All else will fall into place. The big picture is to never seek to fix perceptions when there is an actual problem. This is akin to a band aid on a gunshot wound! It won't work! So kids, please don't try deception at home.

Being more aware of image and etiquette will make you more empathetic.

When you work to become more aware of yourself and what makes you tick, the more you are able to concentrate on and pick up the habits of those around you. A cool side effect is that you will also grow more empathetic and thus be able to know, almost psychically, what those around you are thinking, and mostly importantly how to relate to them. This is an invaluable skill for those who aspire to become leaders of other men. Being able to know what drives other people and the ability to see the world through their eyes can separate you from the masses. That's because the lack of this trait is exactly how people are able to commit cruel and senseless acts against others. They simply aren't using their imaginations to take a few steps in someone else's shoes.

🔍 Millionaire Mannerism:

Seeing the world through someone else's eyes is the best use of imagination there is.

As you hone this skill you will actually see yourself becoming more sensitive to the feelings of others. As men in this world, and because the world can be a cold, cruel and harsh place, we are sometimes taught that being sensitive is a bad thing. This is absolutely not the case. Being sensitive and knowing what others need is a priceless trait. Also think of it as training for when you have a daughter. Imagine raising a daughter –one day-- whose feelings you ignore. . It won't be long before she stops coming to you, and starts going to a different man for her to be able to share those feelings, a sensitive man. See where this is going? Sensitivity, empathy and being conscious of the feelings of those around you go hand in hand, and will keep you in an elite class of people for life.

Millionaire habits form the foundation of the world's most transferable and valuable skill: sales.

We've spoken generally so far about how being an ambassador for Millionaire Manners and an expert in etiquette will separate you from everyone else in the room, but let's talk a little more specifically about how these skills will separate you and your results in the world's highest paying profession; sales. What most people don't realize, especially those who think they hate sales, is that they have been selling their whole lives, with many different degrees of success. Think about it, every time you go to a job interview you are selling yourself. If you aren't old enough to have a job, and you want something from your parents, you sell them on the benefits of buying you whatever it is you want. Trying to get a date? Yep, selling yourself again. Attempting to explain to the store manager of your local electronics store why they should give you a discount? Yes, even then you are selling your point of view. And I mean there are literally thousands more examples in our daily lives of why selling and knowing the basics of sales is so important.

We've gone over these three small words already, but I'll say it once more in a different context. People do business with and buy from those they know, like and trust.

🔍 Millionaire Mannerism:

People do business with, and buy from those that they know, like and trust.

There it is one more time, those three magic words. Learning these skills will make people feel more at ease with you, and in turn more likely to be open to listening to your sales pitch. By being an excellent listener and conversationalist, you are encouraging rapport building, which leads to trust, and ultimately to someone saying they know you, and from there form an excellent perception of you, which they will then spread around for you. Your job is then to live up to those perceptions and watch your referral dollars pour in. Of course, it all begins with you making the conscious decision to pursue this information with heart.

How are people with bad manners perceived?

While we are still on the subject of perceptions, let's take a moment once again to think of some of the adjectives we sometimes unfairly and without merit, use to describe people we perceive as rude. We call them names like trashy, we think of them as uneducated, we say they have no couth, we threaten our children that they should never bring home a person like that, we think they have no home training, and many more awful things. Take the opportunity to think of this book, and all accompanying materials as your own home training program, courtesy of Millionaire Manners! We also want to keep in mind that none of these may be true at all, but it will not stop people from thinking it about them (or us if we don't consistently use this material). The only thing it proves is that these people haven't had the opportunity or inspiration to better themselves in the area of their own etiquette. This is usually because people confuse this type of information with subjects like calculus, or quantum physics, or any of the world's other mysteries. Not so! All it takes to master this information is an open mind, a willingness to change, and a desire to change perceptions that may have been limiting you and your growth for a really long time.

People who are seen as mean, careless or insensitive aren't the people that usually get showered with affection and opportunity. However, this isn't to say this book is all about turning you into some fluffy teddy bear that people can walk all over. This material takes discipline and self-confidence to master, and those are polar opposites of being a pushover. As a matter of fact, later in this same book, I illustrate how this information will ensure you are never bullied again. This information will help you with building your self-confidence even higher, helping make sure you are never pushed over, walked over, or talked over again. This is Millionaire Manners, not a guide to becoming a doormat. That, I guarantee!

How people without Millionaire Manners fare in life.

And now that we know how those rude people are perceived, what sorts of things do they miss out on? Because we know that no one intentionally subjects themselves to the physical presence of negative individuals, we must also know that as soon as a decision maker has the opportunity to balance the scales out in terms of a positive in place of a negative one, I think you have an idea of what that decision maker would do. This is again, because of the fact that these principles are steeped in positivity that radiates outwardly and causes a glow of attraction around its practitioners. Positivity is a force that makes people smile, sets them at ease and usually makes them happier, and thus want to join in whatever that positive person is involved with. When we see those cases where people run from positivity, understand that those are the negative people who need you more than ever. To those people, I say "kill them with kindness," meaning kill their negativity until they are reborn as the positive alliances you need.

Rude people are perceived as not being leaders, because they rarely speak their minds and when they do, their opinions are covered with negativity. Because they are not seen as leaders, opportunities for advancement pass them by frequently, and usually they have no idea. What's even worse is that they are seen as selfish, non-team players. In any professional field or team environment, this is seen as a kiss of death and no one will be looking to you for much. Your attitude is the key to turning it around.

What does it take to train yourself on using these techniques?

In order for you to truly master this information there are several factors involved. We've briefly touched on several, but here I'll go a bit more in-depth. The two that we have already spoken about are discipline and action. You have to be committed in order for this information to work for you. Another factor we haven't spent much time discussing is enthusiasm and how your personal attitude toward the material will determine your success at mastering it. Enthusiasm is approaching a situation with a combination of positivity and passion. One of these alone can be pretty powerful, yet when you combine them, you get the cocktail called enthusiasm. Just think of the people you know who are positive and optimistic people, but don't really take action, yet they always reassure you things will work out alright. We love and appreciate these people, but a closer look will reveal that sometimes these are just words. Then you have the people who aren't necessarily optimistic individuals but you see them light up when they talk about what they love to do, or how much they are enjoying their new project. Now take the two and combine them, and you have one of life's secret ingredients to success. Try it and see!

🔍 Millionaire Mannerism:

Positivity + Passion = Enthusiasm.

The next little discussed factor thus far is value. What value do you place on the material's potential to help you? If anything you've read so far resonates with you, then the potential value is going up for you. But if the book hasn't resonated so far, then the potential value is low. I challenge you as the reader to keep an open mind about what value you can achieve until the very end. You don't go to college and expect a degree after your first semester, and likewise you shouldn't expect to become an expert in etiquette after only a few chapters. But it will happen with patience and work.

There are at least two other areas to keep in mind when studying this information. The first one is simply who do you listen to? This might seem very simple, but you may be surprised at the number of people who take advice from those who don't have a single physical thing or personality trait that you want. If you haven't ever heard this statement before, please let it sink in. If you have heard it before, please revisit it and make sure it's true right now for you more than ever: Never, ever take advice from someone who doesn't have something you want. If you wouldn't take medical advice from the guy who changes your oil, why would you listen to life advice from the person who is at the same level or worse off than you? And I don't just mean financially. I mean professionally and spiritually. If the person you get your perspective from on sports hasn't ever coached or played, or if he's giving you advice on how to be happy yet he's miserable, fire this advisor immediately! He's weighing you down, and you may not even know it!

◎ Millionaire Mannerism:

Never, ever take advice from someone who doesn't have something you want.

The last point on training yourself to use these techniques is understanding what is called the "Teachability Index." The TI is made up of two measurements: (a) your willingness to learn and (b) your willingness to accept change. The beautiful thing is that this concept is not just for Millionaire Manners, it can and should be applied to all areas of your life. Your willingness to change has to do with what you are willing to invest in time, money and effort, as well as considering exactly what you are willing to do differently or give up in order to change for the better. When the two factors are multiplied you get your own, personal teachability index number. The two factors are measured on a scale of one to ten, with ten being the highest willingness to learn and willingness to change. Therefore if you have an eight willingness to learn and a six willingness to change, then your TI = forty-eight, not very good. But if you are an eight and a nine, this is much better, and it shows your internal commitment to getting better. An entire chapter of this book could be dedicated to this concept alone, but this is just an overview so you have something to refer back to later. Always think, how teachable am I? The answer will determine your success both with this material and in life.

Change your reputation today.

Everything you've read so far has to do with reshaping you. Turning you into a better employee, father, leader, manager, husband, etc. All the different roles we play and how people see us in them make up our reputation. As Tony Montana said in the classic Scarface, "I only have my @#$% and my word, and I don't break 'em for nobody." I suspect that Tony was referring to keeping his reputation clean no matter the circumstances, and the fact is that he stated he was willing to die for his. Are you so protective of your own reputation? What are you willing to do to protect yours? I suppose you don't have to go quite as far as Tony Montana, but you should be as equally serious about ensuring that you never have to talk about yourself or your own results or achievements. You want your reputation to "precede" you. That means it comes before you, and can even stand alone if need be. Reading this book is the first step in making sure your reputation is impeccable and that your name is a seal of approval. Millionaire Manners will get you there.

> **⊚ Millionaire Mannerism:**
>
> **When you talk about yourself that's called bragging, when others talk about you, that's called a reputation.**

Millionaire Morals:

- These are skills to help you win in life, not just in one area.
- Good manners have their roots in spirituality and should be taken seriously.
- Your attitude affects everything you do; how's yours?

Action:

1. Check your attitude right now. Is it positive or negative?
2. Ask someone close to you, whose opinion you trust, what your reputation is. Write it down. (We will revisit this later.)

CHAPTER 3

Smile.

Why smile and what it says about you.

It's time Millionaire Manners Ambassadors! You've got your teachability index on 100, your attitude is tuned to receive and you're enthusiastic about being better! Here's your first official Millionaire Manners lesson: Smile. Whew! Just when you thought the info was getting tough! Let me be the first to tell you that this information is fun, and should be fun. You should wake up after having v read or re-read a chapter of this book and feel good about yourself. And then what should you do? Smile again!

Smiling is one of the most underrated things you can do every single day. And not just once a day either, I'm talking multiple times a day and with feeling. This is different than laughing, which is all its own medicine and definitely a topic we will discuss later, but I mean just smiling as much as you can is your first lesson. Question. How many rich people do you see frowning? Just as a general rule, these people are usually pretty happy individuals, at least outwardly. It's usually people who aren't in control of their emotions, circumstances, lives or a combination of all three who just walk around with blank stares on their faces. I challenge you to think about how many times, without being prompted that you smile daily. Keep the answer to yourself for now. But here's the first tip about smiling: every day when you wake up, smile and say thank you out loud, to The Creator, for allowing you another day, because yesterday was someone's last.

⊕ Millionaire Mannerism:

Every day you wake up, smile, and thank The Creator for another day to win.

Those who smile and combine their smiles with a pleasant demeanor exude confidence to all those they come in contact with. It says that they are in control of their own destinies, and that they won't be rattled, shaken or knocked off their games easily. We smile when we have everything under control. This is a tried and true habit of the successful. And please don't take my word for this or any other ideal, principle, rule, notion or assertion in this book. Do your own independent research on everything I tell you, or at least conduct an "eyeball poll" and simply observe some of the successful people you interact with. Of course, there are many definitions of success, but for our purposes let's just call these successful people owners of what you want, and watch them and take notes.

And what happens chemically in our bodies when we smile? When we smile our brain actually releases the chemical hormone called endorphin into our bloodstream, which is responsible for helping us feel pleasure. In turn these endorphins naturally help us combat stress whenever they are released. As it is, smiling is a lot cheaper than antidepressant medication!

Smiling will make you more attractive and inviting.

Smiling much more than you currently do will also begin to allow you to project a much bigger, better more centered ego and self-image. Remember how important self-image is. When

34

you feel good about yourself, everyone else will too. Smiling has this effect. It makes you more inviting, appealing and more attractive than those who don't. You will immediately see the difference when the compliments start coming your way. And if you don't believe me, ask yourself when was the last time you heard someone say, "Wow, what a beautiful frown you have?" Exactly, never! Because no one, and I mean no one (except the other angry and negative folks) wants to be around a person who frowns a lot any more than they have to. I'll also tell you another secret. Those who frown, typically want the same reaction from other people we just discussed. They don't really like themselves, generally speaking, so as a result they use their well-honed negative energy to send out a signal to all those who come in contact with them, "Stay away because I have nothing to offer and I really don't feel that good about myself." Now I know that may sound harsh, but again, look around you, observe, and see what you uncover. I've generalized a bit here, but trust me, it's not too far off. Meanwhile you can say the exact opposite with simply a smile.

🔘 Millionaire Mannerism:

Smiling is an inexpensive way to improve your looks!

Smiling is the foundation for Millionaire Manners.

Smiling is also the first lesson in Millionaire Manners, because it represents the foundation for all other information. Imagine a habit so powerful that it actually changes your body for the better each time it happens. This is the power of smiling. Definitely not to be taken lightly, unless you're smiling. We'll continue to explore all the additional benefits of smiling, but know that combining any of the other habits in this book are absolutely powerful and will transform you into a force to be reckoned with.

The mirror effect.

What we've been discussing so far about attracting or repelling those around you with simply your attitude and/or smile can all fall under the category of another concept called the mirror effect. It basically states that naturally, and usually subconsciously we mimic the demeanor, sentiment, emotion and even physical body movements of those we closely interact with. Wouldn't you rather be the object of mimicry versus the other way around? The flipside of the coin is imagining what happens to those who have no idea of the concept of controlling their own emotions, let alone giving those around you enough inspiration to change their own behavior. Something to think about right? One other way to think of this idea is that in peer pressure, you can either be the peer applying the pressure (positively of course) or the peer being pressured. Which would you choose?

⊛ Millionaire Mannerism:

In peer pressure, strive to be the one applying the pressure, not the one being pressured.

Why are some people happier than others?

Have you ever wondered why some people you know and come in contact with just seem so much happier than other people you know? Do you think it is automatically because they are better looking, have more money than you or are smarter? Any of these could be true, but there's no way to truly tell just by meeting them, and none of these factors alone will make anyone that much happier than the next person. As a matter of fact there are millions of beautiful people running around as you read this who are absolutely miserable because they hate themselves. But what I know, and what you'll soon agree with me on, is that these people seem so much happier because they are so much happier, but not for the reason you think. It's because they've made an actual choice to be the happiest person they know, and as a result are now the happiest person you know too. Amazing how that happened right?

One of the other main factors that goes into the pot of happiness for these individuals is the fact that they actually practice being happy. This dark art includes smiling, giving compliments and having kind words for everyone you come into contact with. What most miserable people don't know about themselves is that they are actually practicing being miserable daily too, and are getting really, really good at it.

The last thing that separates these people from everyone else is that they purposefully and actually purposely look for those things in their day-to-day lives that bring them enough joy to be able to have enough to share with you and I. Isn't that the way you want your manners to shine through?

Are you happy because you smile or do you smile because you're happy?

Psychologists since the beginning of time have been having a number of debates. One of the more popular questions is still what came first; the chicken or the egg? And while this is still one of life's great evolutionary mysteries, another remains that is equally intriguing and a bit more practical, and that is: Do we smile because we're happy, or are we happy because we smile? This may seem, again, somewhat elementary, but I can tell you that your school of thought on this particular question can make a world of difference in your life. And because I'm posing this question to you, the reader, after some time, you can probably guess which side of the coin I fall on and recommend you explore. That's right, I believe smiling will make you happy a lot easier than waiting to get happy and then smiling will. It all comes back to you making a conscious and well thought out decision to simply smile and in turn be happy.

> ### 🖱 Millionaire Mannerism:
> **Smile first, ask questions later.**

The other side of this coin, is much like we've been discussing up to this point, but let's be crystal clear. There's another old saying, and that is "garbage in, garbage out," meaning whatever you put into a situation is exactly what you'll get out of it in return.

What are the different forms of smiling?

I bet when you started reading this chapter you thought that we were only going to be discussing the most common known form of smiling, and that's with our face. Well newsflash, there are at least two other types of smiling that once you master, you'll be well on your way. That first uncommon type of smiling is with your voice. How many times have you spoken to someone on the phone or in person and their voice is monotone, and sounds the same the entire time. They use no variation, inflection or energy when they speak, and for this they usually make us want to jump off a bridge by the time we are done listening to them. The good news is you can always call these type of people when you can't sleep. Get my drift? If you want to learn how to smile with your voice, simply practice not speaking on one notch. That's right, remember one of the magic words we've already talked about; enthusiasm! Remember I told you that when you combine enthusiasm and literally anything else you will come out of the situation better. This is no different. Smiling while speaking, plus enthusiasm equals smiling with your voice. Try that the next time you're on the phone with someone you don't want to speak with, and see if you can get them to mirror you!

The next little known smiling tip is learning to smile with your eyes. This also sounds strange I'm sure, but trust me it works wonders. When you are smiling at someone, make sure you look right into their eyes, and literally make the same motion with your eyes as you do with your mouth and face. It might feel strange at first (even as strange as it sounds) but try it anyway and you will feel yourself engaging in a much fuller interaction with the person you are greeting.

What is the GHP?

Let's switch gears for just a moment and talk about something that might blow your mind. Sociologists are now measuring what's called Gross Happiness Product (GHP) or how much happiness per capita that each of us has in our daily lives. A sociologist by the name of Ron Gutman is studying the science of the smile and its impact, among other factors, on our total GHP. He's outlined many fun facts about smiles:

- Did you know that we can detect smiles at double the distance from which we can distinguish other facial expressions?
- A single smile, given or received, can pack the dopamine load (dopamine is another brain chemical that signals to us we're about to receive pleasure) of 2000 chocolate bars, or the head rush equivalent of winning $25,000.
- It's physically easier to smile than frown; 33 muscles to frown versus only 17 to smile.
- Smiling is actually as contagious as yawning.
- Smiling can reduce your blood pressure.

Ultimately what all this information tells us is: Smile more. You will feel happier, healthier and generally better overall if you are concentrating on those things that make you happy versus those things that upset you. Also, by taking the idea of GHP to heart, we can also invoke one of the world's most accurate laws of science, and that is Pearson's Law. Pearson's Law simply states: "That which is measured improves; that which is measured and reported improves exponentially." This simply means that if we choose to measure our own happiness on a daily, weekly, monthly or yearly basis, it will improve because we are taking time to make sure it does.

> ### 🖲 Millionaire Mannerism:
> **"That which is measured improves; that which is measured and reported improves exponentially."**

The mysterious case of the disappearing smile.

What is the disappearing smile you ask? Let me tell you. You've seen it before, while in line at the grocery store and someone who is trying to be polite glances at you and flashes a weak, curled lip expression which resembles a smile. You can't really be sure because it disappears as quickly as it appeared in the first place. It happened so quickly you can't really be sure it was even there at all. How does this type of smile make you feel, I ask? Empty, without emotion, because that's exactly what this smile was delivered with from its owner. I beg of everyone reading this book, to never, ever give a disappearing smile. I recommend that on those days instead of giving one of these, that you simply avoid eye contact altogether with that person in line behind you rather than give them your empty smile vessel of nothingness. I honestly feel that one of these disappearing smiles is as harmful, though unintentionally, as a frown or no greeting at all. I feel this way because the deliverer is almost giving another person the same greeting they would give a dog or other animal. I say this because you don't really expect a dog to react to your greeting and don't expect the dog to know you didn't really mean it. Therefore I take it as an insult. I'd much rather be ignored personally, than be treated like a dog. At least then I know one of two things immediately; either that person is having a bad day, or they're just plain rude!

Either way, I implore you once more to never give the disappearing smile to anyone, even when you're feeling down. Either try to smile your way back into the game before going into a situation where there will be other humans around, or avoid it altogether. Not doing so can risk your reputation.

How you can tell your smile is actually a smile.

If your whole body, being and aura does not feel good during or after your smile, you aren't really smiling. When a smile is working you whole body engages in the act and everyone within a couple of feet of you will know it too. One thing we've only briefly touched on is energy, more commonly known as vibes. Vibes are our sixth sense's language, or the language of our "guts." We've all been around someone who, within five minutes, gives you the clearest vibes to stay away. Then only a few days or weeks later you hear from a friend some confirmation that that same individual did something to someone that you knew they would do. This is because their energy was off. Smiling is a way of instantly leveling out our energy and balancing the scale when we might be in a negative energy slump. It's natural to have one every now and again, because we all do. What's not natural or okay, is to stay there for an extended period of time, or to bring others down with you. So now that you are armed with this info, it's especially not ok for you! Instead you should be attempting to keep your vibes positive and energy as high as you can so have enough to spread around to those in need when the occasion arises. The way to do this is to smile!

What happens when I'm in such a bad mood I have nothing to smile about?

Great question, and I have an answer for that too! Simply refer to your Dandelion List. Oh, what is a Dandelion List?

Let me explain. As we referred to him earlier, and in his book "Smile: The Astonishing Powers of a Simple Act," author Ron Gutman describes the Dandelion List as basically a short mental or handwritten list of all things you associate with smiling! What an amazing idea. This list can include any and everything that is near and dear to you, with only one requirement: They must make you smile. For me, that's my children when they are laughing (not beating each other up), beautiful scenes in nature, great food, my warm bed after a productive day, memories of licking the spoon after my mother made cookies, and many, many others. All these things make me smile every single time.

Memories are the only thing that survives forever to prove that we actually did a thing and/or enjoyed it (if it was even worth remembering at all). Therefore cherish the great ones you have and put them to good use on a rainy day. This is also a great exercise to complete with any loved one as well, as you will probably identify several shared experiences that can actually go on each other's lists to further solidify a bond between people. Take the time to write yours today!

Why in the world did you dedicate an entire chapter on smiling?

This is an easy question to answer, but before I give you a few more thoughts on smiling before and we move on with this book, here's a question for you. What would a world without smiles or laughter feel like? Take a moment to ponder that. If you feel like I feel and got a chill (not a good one) thinking of the answer to that question, then make a pact with yourself to never again take for granted your Creator-given right to smile. To smile every day at whatever brings you joy. To smile when you remember a funny joke. To smile when you think of your loved one smiling at you. To smile when thinking about how thankful we are to be alive and have opportunities every day to be better than the day before, and so many other things! Smile because you woke up this morning with a purpose and will do whatever it takes to achieve it.

Millionaire Morals:

- There is way more to smiling than you thought right?
- Smiling can change your whole day for the better, and for those around you too.

Action:

1. Practice smiling with your entire body in the mirror.
2. Write out your Dandelion List and keep it with you.
3. Oh yeah, Smile!

PART TWO:
IMAGE

CHAPTER 4

First impressions.

The 12x12x12 Rule.

This where we start getting into the meat of Millionaire Manners principles, where we begin the discussion of first impressions. We've already briefly touched on the concept of the halo effect and how using these techniques and principles will immediately separate you from everyone else in a major way.

The first principle in this chapter is called the 12x12x12 rule. This stands for how you look from 12 feet away, what you look and smell like at 12 inches, and lastly what you say as your first 12 words. In short, 12 feet, 12 inches, 12 words. This is usually the foundation for making a great first impression. That's right, it's **the** first impression we're speaking of here, the one that you only get one chance to make. Now before you go and start feeling pressured by this thought, relax. You'll have plenty of opportunities to add to the excitement and credibility of your reputation. However, this first meeting is the best time to put your stamp onto the blank canvas that is someone else's mind. This is your chance to put whatever you want there. This is one of the reasons why it's so important to look your best, or at least look like you wouldn't be ashamed to run into one of your idols, your boss, or that female you have your eyes on.

⚜ Millionaire Mannerism:

When you first meet someone, now is the time to have them think exactly what you want them to, about you!

From 12 feet away:

- Make sure you have on clean clothes with no obvious stains, discolorations, etc.
- Make sure you are neat, have your shirt tucked in (if you mean to), your zipper up, etc.
- This is a great time to check your posture (which we will examine in-depth later).

From 12 inches away:

- Check your breath (do you need a piece of gum or a mint?).
- Have you been walking around outside all day before going to a meeting, and smell like it?
- Is there anything stuck in your teeth from after lunch?
- Are your hands sweaty?

First 12 words:

- Are you smiling?
- Do you greet the person warmly?
- Are you making eye contact?

The 12x12x12 rule is a simple way to remember that first impressions are absolutely critical, and a quick way to remember that all eyes are on you while you do it. Here's a hint: even if all eyes really aren't on you, act like it anyway.

Why eye contact is so important.

Eye contact during a first meeting is as almost as important as your smile and greeting, and you already know how important I think smiling is. Eye contact tells the person on the other end that you are glad to meet *them,* not everyone else. You make this distinction by making sure you focus your gaze solely on them. Even though you may be equally as happy to see everyone else in the room, don't tell anyone this with your eyes. Eye contact is also one of those tricks that when you practice it, helps you overcome many of the fears and anxieties that are commonly associated with meeting new people, specifically in different social settings. Meeting and keeping someone's gaze is a quick and easy way to let someone know that you are comfortable, even though you may not be, and that you are not intimidated in what may otherwise be an intimidating situation. And we already know the more you can trick your brain into thinking you are good in these situations, the better you will actually be...

Lastly, eye contact takes courage and never really gets less uncomfortable. It does get easier over time as you practice to think less about the discomfort of it, but this discomfort never goes away completely. Let eye contact be one of those games you play against yourself to see how long you can make eye contact and keep a gaze with another person until they're so uncomfortable they look away. Sounds awkward but it really helps. When that other person looks away it's almost as if you've won a small battle that will and should have you feeling more confident and comfortable right away.

🔎 Millionaire Mannerism:

Eye contact + a warm smile = happy to meet someone.

The dead fish. Dry your hands!

As you read the lessons presented in this book, keep in mind that this information is just as much about what to do as it is about what **not** to do. One of the easiest ways to turn someone off and have a person build a negative perception of you is with a weak handshake. When in doubt, always go with more power than less in the all-important handshake contest. Something especially important to note is to make sure you shake a woman's hand with the same force and seriousness that you'd shake a man's. My philosophy on this is simple: We have more women in the workplace than ever before, and at higher levels than we've ever seen in corporate America, with some of these women being just as aggressive as, or even more so than their male counterparts. Many women who do not receive a strong handshake from a man immediately think one of two things: This man is not serious about his profession/life/impression, or he does not take me seriously as an equal/supervisor/colleague. Harsh, I know, but this is reality. There's no quicker way for you to start building a not-so-great reputation than to shake someone's hand without your heart!

🖺 Millionaire Mannerism:
Real friends don't let friends give dead fish handshakes.

The art is simple. Make sure your hand is dry (really important). If they get clammy, extend your hand, get a good grasp of their's and let the valley where your thumb and index finger meet (I call this your hand web) go right to their web. Shake vigorously two to three times, but not more and conclude with another smile or greeting such as "Great to meet you," or "I've heard so much about you," and voila, your handshake is complete. Squeeze a little harder than you think you should and you know you've probably given just the right amount of pressure. I've found that people typically give too little for sake of not coming off too aggressive. It's better to come off too aggressive than to have to fight uphill because they think you're not up to snuff based on your weak handshake.

Remember, no dead fish! The dead fish is the worst handshake known to man, and yet it is still being perpetrated among grown men as an actual handshake during professional and casual meetings. It is the handshake equivalent of ramen noodles without the flavor packet being added in. You know the noodles are supposed to be a meal, but without the flavor packet it just doesn't work. This is when someone simply offers their cold, clammy, limp and seemingly dead hand toward you for the act of a handshake. I won't go on any further, but please do yourself a favor and never shake hands with anyone using the dead fish. If you think you could be guilty of the dead fish at any level, no matter your age, have someone you know who gives firm handshakes evaluate yours. You'll thank me later.

The power of breath mints.

I'll do us all a favor and cut right to the chase on this sensitive topic. This is one of those situations where unless you have the most open relationship ever with a person, he or she will not tell you that you have bad breath. You have to assume that you do and be prepared to act swiftly and decisively to make sure this is never an issue for you. First, make sure you are on a strict regimen of brushing and flossing at least twice daily. Brush before you check email, read the paper, or drink a cup of coffee. Please note that coffee and bad breath first thing in the morning is second only to maybe getting sprayed in the face by a skunk. Even if you're running errands and haven't showered, always brush first! If you're anal like me, then feel free to carry floss with you and floss after every meal. I even had a colleague once who brushed after lunch, in the office restroom every day. That's commitment. If this isn't the level you're on yet, no problem, because the basics work just fine here. Next, go to the store and buy a few packs of gum. Put one anywhere you spend significant amounts of time. That would mean your car, your desk at work, your book bag or briefcase, your favorite jacket, or any other place I've forgotten. Failure to do this can have implications for all different parts of your life, i.e. with members of the opposite sex giving you no attention, people less willing to talk to you about private matters, or people just flat-out avoiding you, all because you haven't been told that you need a mint. This topic also makes people smile because it's somewhat funny, but what isn't funny is what happens when this is left unchecked.

🖢 Millionaire Mannerism:

Just assume you have bad breath and that everyone knows except you. Now fix it!

Not to spend much more time on this topic, make sure you build a good routine for dental hygiene in general, besides the potentially temporary fix of gum. Make sure you brush and floss twice per day. I will tell you that I personally look forward to flossing daily and getting the grit and grime off my teeth. If you have flossed recently and seen the grit and grime that is present on floss when you finish, then imagine what happens when you don't floss and all that gunk stays on or in between your teeth. Gross! So again, brush and floss day and night, and gum. Lots of gum, everywhere, and you will be better for it!

Disclaimer: If gum isn't your thing, feel free to substitute the word "mint" where I have used "gum" and results will remain the same. Fresh, confident breath all day.

The most powerful $30 monthly investment.

For the life of me, I can never understand why people put so much time and energy into their personal belongings, toys and trinkets and then put so little into themselves. I know people who wash their cars every week like clockwork, cut their grass every two weeks, and some who have all the latest electronic gadgets that I've only read about. Yet some of these same individuals haven't learned the value of a $30 investment and what it will do for their reputations, and self-image. The investment

I'm talking about is haircuts at least twice a month. This is all connected to personal grooming and what it immediately says about you. Now I know there are certain trends in both pro sports and among celebrities in general where grunge is coming back en vogue, but the desire to grow a beard does not, and should not come at the expense of good grooming habits. And no one said that when you grow a beard it shouldn't be shaped or trimmed! I also know that some workplaces are more lax today than ever before, and the once stringent dress codes of years past no longer apply. For these situations it's always best to go on the side of doing a little more than what's required. In turn, you'll receive a little extra attention from the folks in your place of business that matter, especially if you deal with customers on a day-to-day basis. Much like smiling will improve the looks of even the toughest looking son of a mother, a nice haircut adds to the calm and confidence of character that you are looking to achieve. Part of this is because of the immediate improvement to self-image that occurs when we look good, and *know* we look good. Don't short yourself on that haircut. Sure, you'll have to cut it again in a couple of weeks, but then again, you'll have to wash your car and mow your grass again soon.

Always start with a compliment.

Another great principle and tool to have in your toolbox is the idea to compliment others as much as possible. Not over the top compliments, or anything to the opposite sex that could be misconstrued as inappropriate or taken out of context, but complimenting a person on something you genuinely like on them, or about them if this is the first time you are meeting that person. For example, you can compliment a person's shoes, or you can compliment a woman's smile. Both would be appropriate, especially when complimenting other men (a plus is when you look your best as well), it makes you appear much more confident in your own skin because although you look good too and know it, you don't mind sharing the praise and/or spotlight with others. It is a subtle show of strength and confidence that goes a long way.

🔖 Millionaire Mannerism:

When complimenting, be as a specific as possible.

Also, you can practice giving unexpected compliments. What I mean by this is, suppose you have been working in the same office for a while now and there is someone who always has nice haircuts, but has started to be taken for granted on this. What better way to potentially make a new friend or ally than to boost their confidence in you by complimenting them out of the blue? Another thing I like to do is compliment women on things that men don't normally notice, and that other women almost always do. For example, I routinely compliment women on their nails instead of their hair, or their shoes instead of just saying they look nice. Another key tip in giving compliments is to be as specific as possible. Saying you love how someone looks in green versus saying you look nice, or telling another man you dig his tie choice today, instead of just saying he looks sharp goes much further in distinguishing you as a classy guy.

At the end of the day, giving compliments is as much about you feeling good about yourself and feeling confident enough to give compliments, as it is about elevating the mood of everyone around you. The more thoughtful your compliments are, the more memorable you become. The more memorable you are and the more you to do improve people's moods around you and edify them, the more they will do the same for you, and be there when you need them.

🔖 Millionaire Mannerism:

Giving a heartfelt compliment is one of the best ways to be remembered.

Your elevator speech.

The elevator speech is your personal thirty second commercial you should have ready whenever prompted with the request, "So tell me a little about yourself." The name is derived from the idea that you should be able to tell someone critical info about yourself, or product in the time it takes to ride an elevator from the lobby, the eighth floor. This is also great to have practiced and have ready because it's usually one of the first questions asked during the job interview. This commercial can also take on different forms. It can strictly highlight you, or it can be a sales pitch that highlights your business or service. Sometimes it can be a combination of all this. No matter what though, there are always some consistent things you want to keep in mind when crafting your pitch. Usually whether or not you are searching for a job is one factor; if not, then you are probably highlighting you and your business for the purpose of securing a lead for the future.

Elevator Pitch Tips

1. It's ok if your pitch sounds a little sales-y. That's because you ultimately want to sell something! Just make sure you are clear on your concept.
2. Make sure you don't include any "huh?" words. These are words or phrases that will make the person you're talking to go "Huh?" which isn't a good thing. Again, be clear and don't include any internal language, or go too high-level or else you will lose them forever.
3. Make sure you've written down your top five most recent achievements at school, your job or personally. This is always great meat to include in your pitch.
4. Avoid using buzzwords or clichés when you speak; words/phrases like "outside of the box," "paradigm shift," or the much maligned "we are the top of _____," unless you truly know everything about your competition.

5. Make sure to ask at least one open-ended question so you're not doing all the talking, and can gauge the interest of the person you're speaking with.
6. Know your business on whatever you're broaching. There's nothing worse than bringing up a topic or statistic then when asked for additional info, you have none. Don't expect a call back.
7. Practice your elevator pitch until it's second nature and you can make the best of those networking events, and actual elevator rides!

🖘 Millionaire Mannerism:

Know thyself, then show thyself!

How to quickly remember names and be remembered.

Ever wonder why some people get remembered in a crowd full of people, and others just blend in and keep getting asked "What was your name again?" Well the answer is simple. First think of all the lessons you've read so far, then realize that any of them by themselves are almost enough right there. But alas, this book is to be utilized altogether, and not just in pieces, in order for maximum results to happen for you. Therefore, smiling, having fresh breath and a firm handshake will do wonders. Combine it with a great elevator speech and some eye contact and you're almost there. Now combine it with this trick and your stock will keep rising. The tip is to say your name as loudly as possible without shouting when meeting someone, then *spell it* for them. That's right, say it then spell it, especially if it's not a common name. If your name happens to be Robert or Michael, try to think of a little tagline to say with your name. Something like Michael from Middleville, or try saying your whole name in a funny, cool sort of way. For instance, Mike Mann from Middleville. They will *always* remember enthusiasm and uniqueness. Have fun with this part and it'll make all the difference when creating a memorable meeting and first impression.

The next tool in your belt is to concentrate on remembering the names of all those people who now remember you! A quick way to do this is to give them their own name tagline, even if they don't give you one. The trick is that you don't necessarily have to say it out loud if it isn't exactly flattering. You may remember Judy as "Moody Judy," (which you probably wouldn't tell Judy) or you can tell her you remember and know her as "Judy the Cutie," which happens to serve as both a name tagline, and a compliment. Two birds with one stone! Combine as many of your tools as you can during everyday situations and you'll quickly become everyone's favorite. The last trick to remembering names is another fun one. Introduce your new friends to as many other people at the event or introduction as possible. Not only will it make you seem like you know way more people than you actually know, you're also getting valuable practice remembering everyone's names. These tips even help if you don't think they're the most important people in the room, because you never know who knows who and whose opinion matters to who.

⊙ Millionaire Mannerism:

Never forget that the sweetest sound in the world is the sound of one's own name. Therefore, remember as many names as you can.

What do you most dislike when you meet someone for the first time?

As we conclude this chapter, use your imagination, close your eyes and go back to every single time you had an awful first meeting with someone and ask yourself, why didn't I like meeting that person? Was it their attitude? Was it their breath? Or was it something you can't quite put your finger on? Picture exactly how that person made you feel with their behavior, word choice, or what they did or didn't do. Chances are though, it was a combination of two or more of these exact points we've discussed in detail that you will use to have a great first meeting, the next time you meet someone for the first time. The cool thing here is that you can start repairing or improving your reputation tomorrow if you use some of these techniques on people you already know. Sort of like what we discussed in the section about the power of complimenting as much as possible.

As you visualize all the things you don't like people to do when you first meet them, take this time right now to make a private pact with yourself that you will never do any of those same things to other people. Be mindful to always give the other person who may do something offensive to you the benefit of the doubt, because as the saying goes, As Malcolm X once said,"There was once a time you didn't know what you know today or think the way you think now." As we learn and integrate information our behavior changes, but we don't want to be the one looking for forgiveness because we made an avoidable mistake. As we know, many people are not that forgiving.

I'll also emphasize the importance of these tools and techniques to our young readers. The art of the first impression is so crucial and an often overlooked topic of discussion among young people, it's one of my favorite workshop topics.. It's also because so much of these lessons are common sense if people just stopped for a moment and thought about what they want to convey in each scenario of their day, or in their lives in general. Make a few small corrections and you are different than everyone around you. How cool is that?

Begin building your reputation with the first impression.

Now to once again take the pressure off, all the lessons we've discussed in this chapter are just some (albeit the most important ones) of the many different techniques you can use for a great first impression, and eventually reputation. Ultimately, in order for a full reputation to build up it takes time, energy and most importantly a commitment to consistency. After all, that's what a reputation is; a promise of reliability, and that you will or should do a certain thing in a certain situation because you've done it before. You'll always have other chances to build or repair your reputation but you only have one shot at the first impression. Cherish this opportunity, and practice on every stranger you meet.

Please also do yourself a favor and don't make the mistake of starting a negative reputation or first impression with a person before you even meet them. In our technologically-driven world, it's much easier than you think to do this. For example, someone, anyone has been trying to reach you for an extended period of time and you finally meet them in person. One of you has some explaining to do, and if you don't use all the tools we've discussed so far and this meeting doesn't go perfectly, you may have lost this person forever. That said, make sure you return phone calls promptly, respond to emails in a timely fashion (which we'll discuss later in detail), and check your social media at least monthly for things you'd feel embarrassed about if your boss saw (which we'll also discuss later). Just think that someone is always watching!

🔍 Millionaire Mannerism:

Try not to mess up a first meeting before it happens!

Millionaire Morals:

- The dead fish is our enemy.
- Breath mints are our friend.

- Your brand depends on you controlling first impressions.
- You have one shot to make a great first impression, so make it count.

Action:

1. Always think 12x12x12.
2. Never leave home without mints and your smile.

CHAPTER 5

What you say before you speak & what your body language is saying for you.

What is body language?

Everyone has heard of body language before, and can pretty loosely define what it is. What most people struggle with however is fixing theirs, and underestimating the impact that poor body language has on their communication strategy and overall personal brand. Truthfully, everyone is saying something before they speak their first word, so it's important that your body language is just as on point as your elevator pitch and grooming.

Body language is typically defined as the process of communicating nonverbally through conscious or unconscious gestures and movements. Meaning, you actually speak with your body and might be completely unaware of it. Just like so many races and battles are won and lost before they begin, the war of communication can begin on sure footing, or lost right in the beginning with the right or wrong combination of body language cues. Let's examine a few of them.

If the everyday words and overall language you speak is English, compare that to the concept of body language. Within the English language, you have hundreds of different *dialects,* or slight variations of English. This means you can be communicating with English to another person yet using a completely different set of slang and colloquialisms to get your point across. This is why the basic language is the same, yet in England, Australia, Ireland, New York City, Minnesota, Canada and dozens of other places, their English sounds completely different.

With body language there are about five main dialects that can either help or hurt your cause depending on how well you practice, and in turn, master them. These body language dialects are: posture; eye contact, smiling, hand gestures, and general facial expressions. Because we've already covered several of these, we'll go right into the ones we haven't.

Posture is a combination of many different parts of the body and how they present your overall message. Posture is sitting, standing and walking combined with how you use your limbs while doing all this.

We've already examined eye contact, but it's important to bring it up once more in the context of what it looks like when combined with the other factors.

Smiling we've also looked at as one of the single most important, if not the most important and controllable factor in building your foundation for success using Millionaire Manners. I repeat, smiling is critical and fun!

Hand gestures are both how you use your hands when you're speaking and how you use your hands when you're not. Many people think the dialect of hand gestures only applies when they are engaged in conversation, but someone sitting still and moving their hands in a certain way is just as telling as frantically moving them around during a conversation.

Lastly, our facial expressions are dead giveaways for when we like, dislike, approve or disapprove all sorts of things, people and situations. You never even have to open your mouth, but if you were put in a situation where all you had was your facial muscles to get your point across, I guarantee you could do it, and do it easily. This is the power of facial expressions.

> ### 🔍 Millionaire Mannerism:
> **Make sure your mouth and body are speaking the same language!**

Ten of the worst body language mistakes.

Now that we've defined both what body language is and what it isn't, let's take a quick look at some of the biggest mistakes people make in their nonverbal communication practices every day. Remember to reflect as you read this list on all the things you can recognize that you, your friends, family and associates/colleagues all do.

1. **Not making eye contact.**
   As it pertains to confidence, and showing confidence when you walk into a room, there are few quicker ways to say "I don't like myself and I'm intimidated easily" than to walk into a room with your eyes looking at the ground. Look straight ahead, and, as I tell my son all the time, walk with purpose!

2. **Slouching when sitting or standing.**
   I'm positive you've heard your mother tell you this at least a thousand times when you were a teenager eating dinner at home, or sitting in your chair, or simply standing around trying to drink a cup of water: "Stand up straight!" I can still hear my mom and dad telling me this all the time, and now I get to tell it to you. Stand up straight! Not only will standing up straight make you look taller, and therefore bigger (remember self-image),

it also conveys that you are confident and have a presence in whatever you do. Imagine this simple trick for growing. Imagine your back against a wall and hold. Instant posture improver!

3. **Giving a dead fish handshake.**
I will spare you, but please never do this. Firm, web, two to three shakes, big smile.

4. **Crossing your arms.**
This is especially bad and telling when you don't actually like what you are experiencing. You don't stand a chance at masking your true feelings if you are frowning and slouching with your arms crossed. Trust me, you will not get invited back to wherever you are so uncomfortable. . Sometimes the best way to enjoy something is to act like you enjoy it. If you still get caught doing this it might just be worse for you. Because you developed this bad habit, you may actually be enjoying yourself, but then someone catches you doing this and thinks otherwise. Try your best to break this habit, and quickly. A good substitute is hands in your pockets, or folded behind your back.

5. **Looking down.**
Again, never walk into a room with your eyes on the ground. Not only might you literally bump into someone, you'll also look bad as you do this. The best place for your eyes is straight ahead or in the eyeballs of the person you are greeting.

6. **Angling your body away from others.**
This is slightly more advanced, but researchers have shown in studies that people are more comfortable and at ease with people who turn into them when they are speaking. This is truly an art, but practice this with friends or loved ones. What will usually happen is that you'll tend to do this naturally for people or subjects you

are truly interested in. The trick is to do it all the time, even when you are only marginally interested in the person or subject they are talking about.

7. **Fidgeting and touching hair.**

   This is especially important when giving speeches or presentations, but can be very distracting during interviews or just normal conversations. People who do this consciously or unconsciously are sending the signal that their hair or hands are way more interesting that whatever the person in front of me is speaking about. Here's another great time to deposit those fidgety hands in a pocket, or keep a glass in your hand in social settings. This way your hands are automatically preoccupied.

8. **Invading others' personal bubble.**

   This is a major offense and a thin line. You want to give the person who is speaking your undivided attention, but you don't want to crowd them. You want to angle toward them, not create an awkward situation. A few quick tips for avoiding this is to first keep 20 inches in your head. This is about the maximum closeness you want to give a person you don't know that well, or are just meeting. The other rule of thumb is moving so close the other person has to take a step back. As long as the other person can hear you, and you them, you're probably at a safe distance. Make sure you check your breath before getting into a deep conversation!

9. **Glancing at the clock.**

   Few things will get you uninvited quicker than staring at the clock or your watch the entire time you're at an event. If you're so important, why did you show up at all? This is the question everyone who sees you will ask themselves.

10. **Frowning or scowling.**
Also pretty self-explanatory, but to drive home the point, the next time you go to the bathroom, stop and frown at yourself and make an observation.

Studies have shown bad posture actually affects your attitude!

As I mentioned before, there is a ton of research on both the pros and cons of having great posture and body language. Another little known fact about posture is that it can actually affect your mood, either negatively or positively depending on how you use it. What's more is that if you perpetually hunch when sitting, or while walking or talking, your entire skeleton begins to change its shape, which is a bad thing when you are slouching or have bad posture. These same studies also show that bad posture can project an attitude of depression or unhappiness, and even low motivation. When you sit up and face the world, your attitude and outlook are automatically improved.

Posture is also key because there is a ton of information on the notion that body language can actually be more expressive than facial expressions, and when the two are put together you don't have a chance to hide what you're thinking, it is there for all to see. Body imaging technology has also been used to study people's individual posture and gait and have concluded that a person's gait and posture is almost as unique to the individual as their fingerprint. Imagine if you had never heard this information before and were just stuck with a bad fingerprint. Instead you now have the power to change something almost as important as your fingerprint, but it's a hundred times more visible!

Now picture your posture as the signature for your body that will signal to people how you feel about yourself, and basically say your name and announce your presence without ever even opening your mouth. The power to control this is completely within you so take advantage of it, and change it for the better. If we choose not to use this universal language to our advantage we run the risk of what basically amounts to cursing out other people with our body language and posture. This is because more research shows that the first language we learned was that of the body and nonverbal communication and cues. This makes perfect sense to think about when we consider that our parents had to glean everything we needed as infants from watching our body language cues. That's right, from the day you were born you have been communicating in this ancient language, communicating your state of pleasure, state of mind, level of hunger, etc. I won't make the mistake of calling a screaming baby a lesson in nonverbal communication, but we can still take these lessons to heart. Because this language is essentially hardwired into each of our minds, not having your body language tuned to the right frequency can result in you turning someone off or upsetting them, and neither you nor they will have any idea what happened. You simply won't get a call back or answer to your inquiry.

Once again, this is me, as your author, imploring that you take the time to approach each opportunity daily to practice, even if just briefly, one or as many of the concepts in this book as possible. We have been learning bad habits, and not learning good ones for so long that without practice, you don't stand a chance at changing permanently. It's you against thousands of years of lackluster programming, but the good news is that you can do it! It just takes practice.

🎙 Millionaire Mannerism:

Body language was the first language known to man; therefore tune your frequency properly to become multilingual.

Your body expresses emotions better than your face sometimes.

We've already discussed that your body is just as capable of expressing emotion as your face is, and depending on the individual maybe even more so. This is why connecting your conscious training and actions to your subconscious programming are so critically important. Whatever you constantly think about and practice will come out when you least expect, through your subconscious, and there will be nothing you can do to stop it. Of course the more aware you are about your own tendencies and those of others, the more you will be equipped to successfully thrive in a variety of situations.

There are two types of posture positions we'll discuss; some that are **powerful** and some that are **powerless.** Which do you think you need to become an expert at? You guessed it, powerful. There's a simple couple of reasons why you don't want to get caught making these type of gestures, or sitting or standing in these type of positions. This is because you consistently should be aiming to project confidence, comfort and control, which we call the 3C Keys of social/professional etiquette. These are in direct opposition to the 3S Keys of poor social/professional etiquette which are scared, submissive, and shaky. You should never project fear onto other people, or tell someone you can't handle a situation. There are some powerful posture positions that are extreme and even convey arrogance, dominance and superiority. We don't want these lessons to be translated into the extreme, because this is just as harmful as the other end of the spectrum. Arrogance as a whole is discussed later in the chapter on true confidence, but the message remains the same. Control your thoughts, do not let others or your subconscious negatively control them for you.

Seven posture killing activities you do daily!

Before we get into the meat of improving your body language and posture permanently, here is a quick list of posture killing activities you probably do daily, and that you should avoid.

a. **Sitting at a computer for extended periods of time.**
   This is one we're pretty much all guilty of, especially if you work at an office and have computer-based work (which is pretty much all of us). Even if you're not taking a bunch of restroom, coffee, or Lord forbid smoke breaks (a horrible habit, and the gum/mint lesson counts double for you guys), just stand right at your desk to get the blood flowing, and even stretch if you have the room to do it. Then sit down and get back to it!

b. **Talking on the phone or texting.**
   Again, this is half of America! We tend to slouch and hunch when talking or texting so this is a tough one. Try to use a headset so you're not holding the phone with your shoulder, which is almost a guarantee for a sore back at the end of the day!

c. **Slouching while driving or leaning too far back in your seat.**
   Especially for our young readers: We are talking to you. It doesn't look quite as cool sitting closer to the steering wheel, but still being able to run a mile when you're forty or fifty is a good trade off.

d. **Wearing overweight book bags or keeping a wallet filled with trash!**
   I don't know how many people I see that are being victimized by one or both of these offenses. Ask yourself what you need for the day, and pack that. Young men, use your lockers to store those extra books, and my older

gents, get rid of those business cards you never used and receipts that expired two years ago. All this does is hurt your posture more while making it awkward for you to sit, ensuring you will have a nice backache later.

e. **Working too much with your arms out in front or bending with too much back.**
Proper lifting techniques dictate you bend at your knees when going down to pick something up, and bringing the load close to your body before carrying it. This put less stress on your back and in turn your posture.

f. **Using your feet inefficiently/wearing poorly supported shoes.**
Wearing poorly supported shoes is a cardinal sin and something that is easily avoidable. If your shoes look cool but aren't the best for long periods of standing, you probably don't want to wear them to an event where you'll be on your feet for hours. This can and will lead to more slouching, or even leaning against things in order to take pressure of your dogs.

Eleven easy tips to improving your body language.

1. **Focus on the position of your feet**: Your feet tell the complete story about whether or not you or others are engaged in the conversation. If they move their torso into you but keep their feet angled away, you're not invited into the conversation. If they point to you, you're in. Make sure you keep these same feet tips in mind.

2. **Smile**: You will be an expert at showing those pearly whites after this book. Be a smile commando and shoot these at everyone!

3. **Practice these power poses**: You can practice these in meetings or in private, or even try them in casual

conversation to determine how they make you feel. In a word, they should make you feel powerful.

   a. Power posture one: while sitting, hands behind your head, feet up on table, call this the **"boss relaxing"** pose.

   b. Power posture two: while standing in front of a table facing others (or imaginary others if practicing), with your arms out in front with your hands open and resting on your fingertips; call this **"boss addressing the room"**

   c. Power posture three: while also standing in front of the room, crowd or participants in front of you, face room with legs wide and hands on waist; call this the **"boss is finished making a point"**

   d. Power posture four: while sitting again, hands behind head, leaning back, one leg crossed over the other; call this the **"boss is waiting while you get to the point"**

   e. Power posture five: while sitting lean back in chair grab the back of the chair next to you and cross legs; call this the **"I'm the boss, tell me all your fears!"**

4. **Align your body**: This tip is directly related to positioning your feet as well, only with this tip you want to concentrate on aligning your entire body with whomever you are speaking with.

5. **Lower your voice**: Unfortunately (unless you have a naturally deep voice), men and women with deeper voices are usually in leadership or management roles because their voices command authority and attention. Through deep breathing practice, you can lower your voice just slightly.

6. **Stretch daily**: This gets the juices flowing inside those little used muscles, if even for a moment.

7. **Deep breathing**: In through the nose, out through the mouth, while you concentrate on standing taller and seeming bigger. It doesn't matter what your actual physical size is, because presence is not about size, it's about state of mind and posture.

8. **Roll shoulders**: Down and back, while moving your shoulder blades toward each other.

9. **Pull your elbows**: Back toward your back pants pockets (your back may crack, this is a good thing).

10. **Wall angels**: Just like snow angels only you can stand up and do these against the wall. It's part stretching, part breathing, all posture improvement.

11. **Stand on your entire foot**: Not just your heels or balls. This one move instantly improves posture and balance.

Millionaire Mannerism:

Presence is not about how big you are physically, it's about how you carry yourself.

Don't play small, play big!

Remember that again, through all these tips and tricks you must keep in mind that you are worthy of whatever praise you receive, and that all the manners and etiquette in the world are only to prepare you to seize opportunity when it is presented to you. Also, we should know this by now yet I'll reiterate it all the same: All the manners and etiquette in the world don't matter without your morals intact. We have continued switching our lessons between internal mechanisms and external mechanisms to ensure they are both growing. Your subconscious can only give back to you later what you've been consciously feeding it while you're awake. We will conclude this chapter with a quick look at the puffer fish. This is a tasty white fish that is fairly exotic, and one that has a good amount of poison inside of it. The puffer fish also has very smooth and colorful skin. However, the puffer fish is no ordinary fish. When it senses danger it actually grows, or "puffs" itself up five to ten times its normal size. Add to this sharp, prickly pointers that stick out when he puffs himself up and this is a serious looking fish! I mention this because I want these lessons to sort of make you into a puffer fish. You are calm now, but when you get caught in uncomfortable situations, I want you to puff up until you no longer sense danger. Then over time you won't sense as much danger because you have practiced all the lessons here. Remember you are only as big on the outside as you are on the inside.

Millionaire Morals:

- Body language is oldest form of communication in history, so study it well.
- You are probably saying more than you realize, and most of it, unintentionally.
- Great posture and body language will improve your attitude, and therefore results.

Action:

1. Look at your posture in the mirror. Now adjust it!
2. Practice two power poses per week for one month. Record results.

CHAPTER 6

Netiquette 101. Many things are temporary but your social network identity is forever.

A lot of information exists in the digital world today

Remember a couple chapters ago we talked about forming your reputation before you meet someone, and how important that can be? Good, because in this day and age it is even more crucial. Just think how when something good or bad happens it can literally spread within a matter of minutes or even seconds depending on who is sending it out and what exactly happened. This is the power of the Internet and the Information Age. The scary part is this sharing of information speeds up exponentially with each successive generation. Once upon a time it took months for a letter to reach its destination, particularly if it was something sent to or from overseas. Then we managed to shorten this to several weeks via mail carriers, trains, and the evolution of the post office. Then we invented the telegram and Morse code to communicate during emergencies and wars and such. Today you can send a tweet or a text all the way around the world and receive a response within seconds! If that doesn't amaze you, just think of all the millions upon millions of years of evolution a single cell phone represents. Circuits and microchips, computer microprocessors, voice technology, and literally thousands of other tiny components are present in every single cell phone in the world.

So what does this mean for the Millionaire Manners Ambassador? It means we are always on our best behavior, and never put ourselves in a position to be made a fool of in front of other people before we even have a chance to meet them. This is the power and responsibility that is at our fingertips in the 2000s. Flying cars will be here in no time! But until then we're stuck with the knowledge that the Internet is history's largest, most comprehensive collection of data ever.

We've all heard of kilobytes (KB), megabytes (MB) and gigabytes (GB), because it's how we measure the size of data. Get this: Research has shown that there is now over 2.7 zettabytes (ZB) of data in existence in the digital world today. To put this into perspective, the average iPod Classic is about 160 GB, enough for about 40,000 songs. 1 ZB is about 1,000,000,000 GB. That's right, one ZB is about 1 billion GB, or the equivalent of more words recorded in every book ever printed. Startling right? What's more startling is the fact that it will never go anywhere, and the fact the experts predict that by 2020 there will be nearly 100 ZB out there! This means we must be careful about what we put out there, unless we want our great grandchildren's kids seeing all the cool (and not so cool) things we did.

🖳 Millionaire Mannerism:
The Internet never forgets.

How does social media and the Internet form your MMC (Millionaire Manner Code)?

So now that you know this huge, crazy mountainous amount of data is floating around in cyberspace, what should you do differently? Well that depends on your current mindset and philosophy regarding online communications and etiquette. I submit that you should use this information to begin forming your e-style. That's right, everyone has an electronic style, only some people have no idea that theirs is telling everyone they know or who reads what they post they are an idiot who has no regard for others' feelings. Fortunately for you, you have Millionaire Manners, and can now intentionally craft your e-style to represent you online as an extension of who you are in real life. I hope this is great news for everyone reading this because we're spending more time online and interacting with our social networks than ever before. But for some people they are completely different online than they are in real life and even take to acting out fantasy personas. For an in-depth look at this topic, I recommend *Virtually You: The Dangerous Powers of the E-Personality* by Elias Aboujaoude.

Let's take a look at some of the more basic rules of online etiquette, or "netiquette."

Millionaire Mannerism:

Your e-personality should be an extension of the real you, not a different you.

Core rules of engagement of netiquette.

We call these few basic items the Rules of Engagement of Netiquette. Read them, absorb them and use them today!

First things first, **we are all humans**, meaning that at our core we simply desire to be treated with love, and at a bare minimum respect. This should absolutely translate online as well. I once heard a notable celebrity speak on why she loathes reality TV. What she said still sticks with me today, and that was her not watching reality TV because in her eyes, it's almost always steeped in and aimed at humiliating and degrading another human being. Sometimes the videos and clips that are the most "popular" are those showing something unfortunate or downright mean happening to someone else. We wouldn't like it if it was our mother, sister or grandmother, yet we let these humiliating things penetrate our psyches until we're numb to the horrible things that happen every day right around us. This is the perfect time to bring up the best "old adage" we might have: "Do unto others as you would have them do unto you." (We will revisit this adage with a slight twist later).

⊛ Millionaire Mannerism:

Do unto others as you would have them do unto you.

Next, and this is one we've already spoken about a bit, you should **use the same personal or moral code online as you use offline.** Again this is about being consistent and building a reputation as a consistent and genuine person. You don't want to act one way here and then act completely different in other environments. You want the type of consistency that people can set their watches to, and that people can rely upon. These are the people that advance in life. Here's a hint: if you don't have a personal/moral code in real life, you should think about that before thinking of an online strategy.

The next tip is also one that again, translates very well from the real world into cyberspace; **always know where in cyberspace you are.** This may seem simple but clicking the send button has got to be one the least contemplated actions of many people's day, and it shows. In other words, if I don't know who is connected to another person I'm connected to, and I want to post something that could be questionable, I probably want to consider my audience and environment **before** I post it. An example of environment would be an online discussion of politics, and I interject a comment or picture on a sports related subject. Everyone who reads it is immediately going to scratch their heads and look at your profile to determine who the bonehead is who can't follow a simple conversation. Simply pay attention to your audience and environment before you post.

One tip or thought that is often overlooked online is to make sure you **respect other people's time, even online.** Keep to the topic at hand. For instance, I've seen Facebook conversations turn bitter and caustic once someone interjects something that had nothing to do with the original topic. Keep it civil. The same thing goes for email. If the person who initiates conversation is keeping their email to two or three lines, it's probably a safe assumption that, unless they request extensive info, they probably want something short back too.

This tip has a definite reversal and/or caveat, because there is an extreme version of this trait, but for the time being **be as much of a resource as you can.** In cyberspace there are a lot of know-it-alls and folks who type just to hear the keyboard click. Therefore if you actually have something to add, all the better. Just make sure you don't turn into a know-it-all.

This is a lesson most us still haven't learned from one of our greatest Presidents, and that is when a man, any man, offends us, we should write a letter to him. One detailing how terrible of a person he is, along with all his faults, and further, why you don't particularly care for him. Abraham Lincoln would write this letter and then promptly throw it away afterwards. It was the exercise alone that always made him feel better about the situation, and most importantly, allowed for his cooler head to prevail. Therefore on email, Facebook, Twitter or anywhere else I beg you to **keep fire balls and flame wars to a minimum!**

Because it's so easy to get information about anyone or anything we wish, it's important to remember and keep in mind that some people don't want to be found or contacted, so make sure you **respect other's privacy.** Just think of those moments when you just want to be left alone and don't want any contact with the outside world. Believe it or not there are actually some who live their entire lives that way and that's perfectly fine. Simply find your balance and let them have theirs.

This should be self-explanatory, but I won't assume anything. I'll just remind us all of one of the great warnings on being mindful of our power: "With great power comes great responsibility." **Don't abuse your power,** because it can easily be taken away. Again, be the same person online as you are in real life. If you wouldn't consider yourself a bully in your day-to-day life, or if you don't condone bullying as a true show of power, why start this behavior online?

As they say, this last item could've easily been number one, and that's the notion of **forgiving other's mistakes because it could be you.** Speaking of true shows of power, that's what being compassionate and forgiving is all about. Anyone can hold a grudge, but it takes a big person to get offended or wronged, get upset, yet still find a reason to forgive so you don't keep paying rent to that person for living in your head!

Google is your new girlfriend's first reference point.

If you need a bit more motivation on why else to keep your profile as much on the up and up as possible, consider this: That cute lady or girl you have your eye on knows how to use the Internet! This means that every time you meet someone for the first time and they don't know you, and have reason to want to know more about you prior to entering into whatever relationship is on the table, the first place they are going to is Google. That's right, the world's favorite search engine is also your potential girlfriend's favorite, as well as her best friend's, and the police department's most accurate informant and the one actual reference potential employers almost always check. I've heard stories of people checking on their significant others' online pasts and been shocked and shamed right out of relationships. I think we've all also heard of these World's Dumbest Criminal types posting pictures of their stolen loot on Instagram, only to have the cops show up in the next five minutes!

One of the most crazy and somewhat sad examples of how online pasts can come back from the dead to haunt the living would be the story of a New York City guidance counselor I read about a couple years back. Here was a respectable, and quite attractive guidance counselor who had worked in the NYC Public School system for years. But one day some of her students thought it would be cool to search the Internet for her to learn more about the woman they all had a crush on. What they discovered actually crushed the young guidance counselor's career. What these young students found out was that their favorite guidance counselor had been a lingerie model prior to her joining the school system, and they found dozens of inappropriate pictures of her online. Now here's where it gets crazy: None of the pictures were nude, and she even had a contract with the website stating that the pictures were to be removed when she left the agency, so technically they should have been long gone. They weren't, and when school officials got wind of the situation they fired her. Now due to teacher's union protocol, after the investigation she was offered full reinstatement, but the damage had already been done. She never returned to the school. Do you think she ever thought anyone would ever find those pictures? I'm willing to bet she had probably forgotten about them altogether, but the Internet didn't. She didn't think twice about it when those pictures went up, but you have the chance to think twice about everything you post. Would you want it to show up ten years from now?

BUSINESS NETIQUETTE

Introduction to email & e-style.

Along with the Internet and being able to access information whenever we want, one of the other major changes that happened about 20 years ago was the advent of electronic mail, or email as a primary means of communication both professionally and socially. Only recently have we been introduced to messaging through Twitter and Facebook, but even these apps have their roots in chat rooms that were created in the mid-90s. As with any new system, it takes time to learn it and what is proper when using it. I'm sure since you are alive in the 2000s that you have already sent thousands of emails in your life, but what this information is about is how you can be better in those normal interactions day-to-day that you completely forget about and/or take for granted, that they can't be improved or that you can't be seen in a different light after taking a few tips to heart.

The main complication and challenge that email presents itself is once again steeped in the fact there is ultimate anonymity associated with it, and secondly that it is so readily available and so easy to use that we underestimate its power. Hundreds of years ago we had to think long and hard before sending a letter because you had to write them first, and then take it to a postman (there weren't many mailboxes at the turn of the twentieth century). Therefore each word was carefully crafted, and its implications upon reaching its intended recipient were thoroughly pondered. Not so anymore. We can have a thought and literally within seconds send it to a person 10,000 miles away. So much of the information presented in this book is about combatting the unintended consequences across the board as it pertains to living in a society of instant gratification. Yes you can type a thank you email, but because everyone uses email, it doesn't carry the same weight. I suggest sending a thank you card in the mail. It has a much different feeling attached when someone takes the time to use a pen and paper. How you decide to use email as a tool will help you in making sure you have a respectable e-style that fits in line with your complete persona and reputation.

The main things to keep in mind are the core rules to netiquette, and always considering what your objective in the communication is. Once you establish what that is, then you can set upon accomplishing that while looking as good as possible. Of course also keeping in mind that **anger, sarcasm, and any other extreme emotions do not translate well in online communication.** Therefore do your best Abe Lincoln impression and try to purge yourself as much as possible from emotions in the short-term when you are trying to get your point across to another human.

Don't ever do these, *aka* the quickest way to get uninvited from everything.

Becoming a Millionaire Manners Ambassador is so much based on respect that it's still a wonder why most folks don't realize to simply follow their instincts for this. This next set of rules are all based on this unalienable right, and that is the one that says just automatically give everyone respect, whether or not they've "earned" it, because you never know. Most important, it's you making that karmic deposit that will surely come back to you ten-fold, one way or the other. That said, here is another quick list of things not to do when sending email:

a. Don't be a predator, meaning don't be a creepy guy who says creepy things. You will probably be reported to the powers that be and develop an awful reputation in the process.

b. Don't create fake personalities. You'd be surprised at the number of people, according to several polls, who actually create fake profiles so they can spy on someone or observe them unnoticed. This is partially related to not being a predator and creep, because this is also very creepy.

c. Don't commit electronic forgery. This may shock you, but a tremendous number of people commit this crime frequently and that is saying you are someone else with the intent to deceive while assuming an actual person's persona. This is not creating a fake account to spy, this is posing as someone else. Highly illegal.

d. Don't forward this message: fwd: fwd: fwd: fwd… Whatever you do, don't be that guy who just figured out how the forward button works and decides to forward obnoxious chain emails. This is *spamming* and it's not a good way to make friends. You will look up and people will stop taking your calls. The good news is that this really doesn't happen to me all that much anymore; instead it's been replaced by the equally obnoxious practice on Facebook or Instagram where someone "tags" a picture of you, that you aren't even in! Talk about obnoxious. I usually unfollow these people ASAP. Yep, even family!

e. Don't spread rumors online. It's so easy and the person you're talking about isn't right in front of you. Don't fall into this trap, because as we've already talked about, the Internet never forgets and there's always someone who has saved what you said about that person you both know. It's not worth it. If you have an issue with someone, cyberspace is the not the place to deal with it.

f. Don't harass or bully: This is another one of issues that has taken off significantly recently. Cyberbullying has become so bad that many youngsters have actually taken their lives as a result of the degree to which they were taunted and humiliated by their peers using social media. The horrible thing is that adults are participating in this same type of behavior at their workplaces, and then turn around and wonder where their kids picked it up. Another one of those good old adages is "If you don't have anything nice to say, don't say anything at all." Your mother would be proud!

g. Don't send worms or viruses because of your negligence. If you are unsure of who sent you something or it's in your spam folder, do yourself and a favor and don't open the message. Then do everyone you know and whose email addresses you have access to a favor as well, and

do not forward that shady looking email. You are putting them and yourself at risk for viruses. She same goes for downloading anything from the Internet from a site you are not familiar with.

Email at work.

The rules you just read flow right into the more specific topic of emailing while at work, which is much different than emailing in your personal life. The stakes are much higher, but luckily the same basic rules still apply. Treat everyone with respect and stay away from extreme forms of emotion, for these almost always land you in trouble. Instead, think of all the good you can do with the *tool* that is email. Remember this is supposed to make your life easier, not harder and more stressful, and that's what some people allow to happen. Here's a couple of basic rules and thoughts for work email.

The effects of email on the working world.

First you must consider what email has done overall to the work world. It has shortened communication time and face time so significantly that many people actually gain weight since they no longer have to leave their desk to go and meet people face to face to get answers. It's also very easy now to reach high-level individuals without being screened, since many of these people check their own email. Next you have to keep in mind that many people send and hide behind the anonymity email provides because they are too scared to have a real face to face conversation with anyone. Lastly, there are some people (who are usually the same people) that both send too much email and simultaneously become overwhelmed by the amount of email they receive. Go figure. Never let email become something to hide behind. Solid reputations are not built on practices like that.

Emailing the CEO and the rest of the company.

One of the first rules of restraint and discretion still stands that just because you can do something, doesn't mean you should. This single lesson has so many practical applications in life in general, but we will stick to the here and now and keep it focused on the topic email conversation. You have some individuals who think because they have their CEO or Director's email that this is some sort of open invitation to just email away. Please don't even think about emailing multiple levels about anything negative either. This is a one way ticket to professional oblivion. Once you have that established, the rules of workplace email pretty much mirror personal ones from here on. And to prove it, here's an interesting story I heard.

Two middle managers at a large computer company, both married to other people, were having an affair. They started sending each other pornographic love notes over the company email system. One day, one of them accidentally sent one of these missives to everyone at company headquarters. They were both fired.

The moral of this story is:

(a) Be faithful to your spouse.

(b) Don't cheat on your spouse on company time.

(c) Don't send anything over email that you wouldn't want published on the front page of *USA Today.*

(d) Delete the "all-at-company-headquarters" alias from your personal address list immediately. This should pretty much never be used.

Dealing with email overload, real & imagined.

A couple rules we've already addressed help with both these issues. The first is email overload, which usually comes from folks that are tied to those who over-communicate (which is pretty subjective). These people copy you unnecessarily, and relay the most mundane of info via their outbound emails. Such niceties as, "I'm gone for the day," or "The copies are in your mailbox," or even "I'm going to make copies," make for full inboxes and an uptight work group. Don't be this guy either. Only send the message if it needs to be sent. This will eliminate actual email overload.

The flip side to this coin is the person in your organization who always seems to get the email late or just simply never responds, leading you to believe they never saw it, or saw it late. These folks haven't come to realize that some email is actually a part of their job, and responding and not responding is also critical in ensuring a business is running properly. These people feel that any email is an unwelcome intrusion so they either don't check it enough, or don't check it at all. This would be imagined email overload, and if you must deal with this individual in your workplace, standard CYA (cover your @$&) tactics apply. Use the return receipt feature on your mail system. If you send an important email and it's not read in a reasonable amount of time, follow-up with a phone call. If you still get nowhere, send another email note and copy your own boss (if you just want to keep yourself out of trouble) or the other person's boss (if you want to get the other person in trouble). Warning: Copy a manager only when it's really important that your information get through. It's a technique guaranteed to make you unpopular with the person you're supposed to be working with, and the boss may see it as evidence that you're not capable of working out your problems on your own. Copying both bosses is almost always overkill. Use discretion here. The cool thing is that you can also simply try to limit the amount of time you spend communicating with this person to begin with.

SOCIAL NETIQUETTE

Netiquette at home: Be present.

One of my favorite areas to speak on is how to remain in the moment when so much technology and opportunity to share everything exists. First, there existed this fun and amazing place before technology and cell phones came to be, and it actually still does. That mythical and magical place is called Earth, and it's as beautiful as ever! Getting kids and some of our loved ones to realize this is an entirely different issue though. The one thing we can control is how we model what we'd like to see present in others. By that I mean if you live alone or with family, or your mate or spouse, enact a no-technology time space within your home. This could be the time you use for writing in your journal and reflecting the day's events, or finding that elusive 15 minutes to read. Whatever you do, for however long you decide on, make sure you put your whole into it and make sure you put the iPad, cell phone, laptop and remote control down and just enjoy time.

This exercise believe it or not, is also great practice for social settings as well. Imagine you're at dinner at a beautiful restaurant with a beautiful woman, or in a meeting, or somewhere else important, and there's the one guy who can't resist checking his phone for Lord knows what, as if he's the only one with responsibilities in the whole room. Don't be this guy! It can also be another one of those body language cues that makes a person look completely uncomfortable or inadequate because their phone must be in their hand! It could also signal to other people that either you are a poor conversationalist, or don't want to be bothered by those who would attempt to engage you. Being able to survive without being plugged in takes a serious and dedicated conscious effort to make happen. We've all been the guy I just described and/or been told by our wives to put the phone down, but now you know why. Because especially when you are with her, it shows a complete lack of interest in her and your quality time together if your phone is a permanent part of the relationship. Put down the phone and enjoy the party.

🔊 Millionaire Mannerism:

Enact in your household a no-technology hour (or more) to engage one another, reflect and just be.

Netiquette at school.

The rules of karma always dictate that in order to be outside of something, or to not have a certain thing come to you, you should make sure that you never do that thing to others. Case in point would be bullying. Like we've already spoken about, technology makes it so much easier to engage people both positively and negatively all around the world. Therefore we should make it a point to use this power for good, not evil. Young people in school and even adults in the workplace should make sure they never engage in bullying of any sort, because it could easily be you or your children getting bullied. The other practical reason, one that we've covered pretty extensively, is because everyone can see exactly how you choose to use your social media power.

Over the last couple years we've seen a sharp rise in the number of suicides by teens and preteens alike as a result of horrific taunting and bullying taking place in these online arenas. Just recently we even heard of an actual NFL player being subjected to the unprofessional and distracting behavior of bullying and taunting. Those with the power to make people feel less than adequate about themselves are the ones who secretly feel the worst about themselves inside. Part of this book's premise is to make you feel so good about being you, that you never feel the need to resort to knocking someone else's self-esteem down in order to build yours up. This is one of the worst forms of low self-esteem and it's perpetrated more and more daily because cowards love fighting behind someone else. In the next chapter we talk about several aspects of building up the confidence and self-esteem needed to face any challenge, including that of holding your Millionaire Manners badge high!

Challenge yourself to be professional and compassionate in all settings, and to go the extra mile in calling this behavior out when you see it. People always remember deeds like that, and they set the stage for your heart to be clean, full and open to receiving your share of the divine pie. You can't lose!

🏵 Millionaire Mannerism:

Challenge yourself to be professional and compassionate no matter the circumstances.

Love and relationships online.

There are few universal languages that translate as well as happiness, a smile or a hug. However, their evil cousins desperation, aggressiveness and anger happen to travel lightly too. These evil cousins are the same ones you want to promptly and unceremoniously erase from your toolbox and repertoire prior to beginning any attempted courtship online. Here's where we go back to e-styles, and some people thinking just because they can type something they would never in a million years actually say out loud, that it's even remotely a good idea to do so. Being genuine online and appearing to be a go with the flow type guy starts with integrating some of these traits into your daily routine now. Women can always sense when a guy is pushy and overly aggressive after a couple pieces of correspondence. Usually by the third or fourth interaction, because most people can't hide their true colors for that long. Therefore here are a couple more tips on crucial mistakes not to make:

a. Don't be too pushy. Like I said, women can smell this a mile away and they run from guys who are pushy, needy and smothery. Be yourself, unless you are a pushy, needy and smothery guy. In that case do what doesn't feel natural and follow her lead.

b. Be yourself. This means don't do or say anything you wouldn't recognize from yourself when you read it tomorrow. Don't hide behind anonymity as if there is no tomorrow, there surely is and you will be alone in it.

Inappropriate material online.

I cannot stress this point enough, but if you are looking at or "happen to come across" inappropriate material on your computer, make sure you do it in private or on a private machine. Needless to say this sort of thing can make everyone uncomfortable and yet it can be completely avoided by exercising a small amount of discretion. And by inappropriate I'm not just talking about adult sites or related material. I'm talking about viewing anything that doesn't really fit into where you are.

Millionaire Morals:

- The internet never forgets.
- Resist the urge to act completely different online than you do in real life.
- Your Millionaire Manners Code must exist even in cyberspace.

Action:

1. Think twice before you post, tweet or hit send.
2. Ask a close friend to review your profile. Write down their description and analyze.

CHAPTER 7
What is True Self-Confidence?

Why is confidence important to having Millionaire Manners?

Confidence is the lifeblood of Millionaire Manners. It is the foundation for everything we've spoken about in this book so far, and will continue to discuss. You can't give a firm handshake, smile or speak with surety unless you have ultimate belief in yourself. However, I know that when coming from a place where we haven't been taught how to be gentlemen, having confidence in yourself in a variety of sticky situations is asking a lot. This is why we've spent a tremendous amount of time iterating and reiterating the different messages associated with practice, repetition and making sure the lessons are practiced in earnest before thinking they didn't work for you. I assure you they will.

The question of having confidence and its visible and invisible impact in our lives is almost as fundamental as wondering why we should even practice this Millionaire Manners stuff at all. Our friends and family who wonder things like this are our most challenging converts in a world where civility has become all but extinct for many, and a luxury for the rest. This practice is looked at as something strange instead of how we live our lives on a day-to-day basis. Having the confidence to be an ambassador goes a very long way when we are trying to impact society on a whole. We must have confidence in ourselves to stay the course, and have the ability to respond when needed, as well as the confidence in ourselves to know this is absolutely the right course to take. Where exactly does this confidence come from? I'm not talking about misguided bravado and machismo that comes from a person who has no fear of consequences, and will act in anyway regardless of social impact, but rather true self-confidence that comes from having the knowledge to react when necessary and respond to whatever stimulI is thrown our way, ensuring we stay above the fray while doing so. This comes from preparation and belief in what you're practicing. Let's keep working on it!

Recognize your insecurities.

One of the coolest steps in furthering your own self-image is somewhat counterintuitive, I admit. That step is to look in the mirror and acknowledge, to yourself, and any of your friends or loved ones whose opinions you value, all your worst traits, faults and insecurities. The immediate feeling you will get after doing this is best compared to the alcoholic or drug addict after they hit rock bottom and finally come to grips with their addiction. Harsh comparison, but the weight that is released from the shoulders of these individuals is worth the pain they experienced on the path of self-discovery, and now pushes them further down this same road toward recovery and healing. While not as extreme, at least not in most cases, the journey to finding one's stride and confidence can be just as taxing, relieving, and ultimately as healing as any other endeavor. It takes a self-aware person to admit any of their own faults, and that is why this is one of the first steps that needs to happen in order for your true confidence to shine through. So please take the time right now to pause your reading, sit the book down, and reflect on what you don't really like about yourself and/or what you don't do that well. Write them down in your journal even.

◉ Millionaire Mannerism:

Knowing and being realistic on what you're not good at is just as important as knowing what you are.

Now that you've taken the time to sit and think, reflect, or even write down some of your negative traits (and remember, we all have them), don't you feel better? Lighter even? If you don't have this feeling, you probably weren't honest with yourself. And if you want my next suggestion, which I only recommend after reflection doesn't work, go ahead and ask that trusted friend or loved one what they don't like about you and see if that helps. Of course one of my favorite sayings applies here without a doubt, "Be careful what you wish for because you just might get it." In all seriousness, as you do this it will become clear what you don't do well or aren't that good at, so now you focus solely on the other side of the coin. Now that these traits or things you didn't know your friends and family felt are now out in the open, you should feel powerful with that knowledge. You have also just done a tremendous job through either asking or sharing your faults with your family, which now leads to them trusting you more and having the faith and freedom to give you feedback on your journey from here on out. This is because people love to be shared to, and love being asked their opinion even more. Please also resist the urge to discount someone's feedback or opinion of you just because they have a bad reputation themselves. One of the truths I've discovered in life is that you can learn from **anyone** and **everyone** if your antenna is up. That person who told 99 lies in a row just might tell the truth about you the 100th time so you better listen up!

> **⊕ Millionaire Mannerism:**
>
> **Just because a person told 99 lies, doesn't mean the 100th one won't be true to you.**

Let's also be crystal clear once more that this entire exercise is about growth for you as a person, and ultimately to build your ego and confidence to a healthy level, and that is sustainable. What this exercise isn't for is for you to dwell on the past and relive all the mistakes you've made, but what should be clear after you take the time to discuss your traits with someone you love and who loves you, is what might lead to your mistakes in the first place. Armed with this information you should be able to make much better decisions going forward. Because you've gone through the bonding process with your inner circle and broken down your "What Others Know and You Don't," window pane (refer to Jo-HarI Window in Chapter 1) you will be that much stronger and confident moving forward in your life. Acknowledge, cleanse, and commit to change!

Identify your strong suits & successes.

The next part of building supreme confidence in one's self is truly one of the most fun parts of the process. Now you get to ask those same friends, associates and confidants to shower upon you all the awesome and more practical traits you possess. Going through this process is a big confidence boost for anyone. It will give you a chance to learn things about yourself that you never knew. As you start hearing the same things from multiple sources, it is probably safe to say that those are probably some of your strongest suits, and ones that you want to make sure you lead off with in any situation. In his (awesome) book *Now, Discover Your Strengths*, author Donald O. Clifton tells us why most don't realize their innate talents, skills and specials traits: "We live with them every day, and they come so easily to us that they cease to be precious."

Don't take your Creator-given attributes for granted, use them to become even better! There's no better way to pay homage and worship the Most High than through utilizing every bit of the ability you were given. To not use it is to not appreciate it.

■ Millionaire Mannerism:

The best way to show your gratitude to The Creator is to use the gifts you were given.

The idea of first knowing exactly what you're good at, i.e. what comes easiest to you, then using those talents more than anything else can seem like an unconventional thought, but in reality this is the best thing for you to do. It gets really weird when you study even more about using your strengths to your advantage because new research actually shows that you have the most opportunity for growth in your area of strength!

Relentlessly practice what you are good at.

Now is a great time to cover the four steps to learning new information, and set a road map and goal for where you want to go with learning yourself, but also in learning the information presented in the book. The four stages are:

Unconscious Incompetence: This stage of the process is where you don't even realize that you don't know something, and represents the most dangerous spot in the quadrant to be in. This new information is only uncovered through being told what you lack, or seeing something that piques the curiosity, but as it stands right now you have no idea about this information.

■ Millionaire Mannerism:

If you're always the smartest person in the room, either go different places or make sure different people are in the room.

Conscious Competence: This stage of the game represents information that you know you know. You might have always been good at this certain set of tasks or activities, or you might have even trained yourself to get proficient, but no matter how you came to know the information you still have to think about it in order to get the tasks done.

Conscious Incompetence: This stage represents when your eyes have been opened and you now actually know that you don't know something of value, and in theory should set out in acquiring that knowledge.

Unconscious Competence: This last stage represents the most desirable spot in the quadrant to be. To land here is the goal of learning anything new, and that you learn it so well that it becomes completely unconscious, in that you don't even have to think about it in order for you to perform excellently. Also known as auto-pilot.

Why did I take the time to outline these? It's not only to give you an idea of how you should approach learning in general, but also to let you know how you should approach learning about you. This chapter is all about establishing genuine self-confidence and, I'll repeat, this can only be built by forgetting about what you're not good at, then discovering what you are good at, through the process we've outline, then practicing it with all your might. Keep practicing until you no longer have to think about it, in order for it to be excellent. The other reason for bringing up the quadrants is to once again make sure that everyone knows there are no perfect human beings walking the planet right now, only works in progress. Ironically, the ones who have the most going for them, i.e. confidence, beauty, talent and more, wholeheartedly embrace this fact. Let's make sure we do as well.

Be thankful daily!

I know you all are probably tired of me giving you so much basic information. That's how I felt when I first began learning and practicing these principles and watched my life change before my eyes. I became lucky, always invited places and well-liked, even loved by many, just because I did what everyone already knew but chose to ignore. The only real knowledge is applied knowledge. Those attempt to collect bits and pieces of information to showcase like trophies don't usually have much else to show off. Now, on the other hand, those who take this information and any other information for that matter, and actually apply it to their lives live a starkly different existence than most other people. It's because they believe in the information and they **practice** it.

🔍 Millionaire Mannerism:

The only knowledge that is power is applied knowledge. All else is just a trophy.

Now we can continue with our regularly scheduled programming. The next item on the road to becoming that confident version of yourself is to take stock of everything you have to be thankful for daily. Similar to your Dandelion List, make sure you have at least a mental list of all the things in your life you love, enjoy, and therefore should be thankful for. If we reflect, this list's contents should be really easy to complete. If you are healthy, please start there, followed by your children, your parents, or both. Your mind, a vocation and any hobbies can also go on this list. One of my favorites is simply opportunity, because when all else fails we each have the opportunity to become a completely new and better person today, but only if we choose it.

The benefits of being thankful is that you will also become more naturally inclined to be gracious of others in those scenarios where discretion is your best option. Being as gracious as possible is a quick way to earn extra deposits in the bank of karma, International. The more you deposit, the higher your

ROI (Return on Investment). But what happens instead is that there are many of us who walk around counting what everyone else has to their name instead of considering the individual who hasn't anything to theirs. As a result, those who are cognizant of what they have and thankful because of it are able to walk with their heads higher, and with good vibrations emanating off from all around. It truly is an amazing factor.

Be positive.

The very close relative of being gracious and thankful is what we call having a positive mental attitude. Feel free to even call this an "attitude of gratitude," related to the last section, and is directly related to being at ease with one's self and surroundings. Make sure we do not confuse this with being complacent or satisfied either. My hope is that you have purchased this book and accompanying material with the sole thought in mind to not remain as you currently are, but to grow, become better, and eventually enrich the lives of those around you through the example you live. Therefore this is the exact opposite of complacency. The concept of positive mental attitude (PMA) is another one that seems fairly simple and straightforward, yet there are many aspects to it which give it the potential to become one of your most powerful allies in the fight against our arch-nemesis, *mediocre manners*. We haven't covered this much so far in the book, but our entire fight is against mediocrity as an institution in society. Many times we are taught to simply do enough to get by or not to not ruffle any feathers, and other ridiculous explanations to not be your best self. Do not read any further if your objective has mistakenly been written down as wanting to blend in or be like those around you. Understand that these teachings will make you somewhat strange. Why is he going out of his way to greet everyone every morning? What is he trying to prove? And one of my favorites: Who does he think he is?

Back to PMA. You are and should think you are a Millionaire Manners Ambassador wherever you go. You should absolutely think that great things are going to happen to you today, not because you did something for someone else necessarily, but because you filled someone's day with joy for free, and as a result you expect good things to happen to you. This is the universal law of value. You cannot give value to those around you in a consistent manner for an extended period of time and not be rewarded handsomely for it. This is the way it works. Nine of the ten richest human beings on the planet are so because they changed the way the world operated, not for worse, but for the better. Expect good things of yourself and those around you and that's exactly what you will get.

Accept compliments graciously.

There is an absolute art to accepting compliments but most people do it all wrong here. Here's the art; accept the compliment! That's right, just take the compliment and simply give one in a return, like a heartfelt, "Thank you!" What usually happens is that out of reflex the person being complimented is either so unused to receiving a genuine compliment that they give the disingenuous knee-jerk and dreaded *return compliment,* or they give some sort of pseudo-smug remark in return like, "I know." Both of these are horrible to do. Let me explain why.

The "knee-jerk return compliment" is the equivalent of someone on your birthday giving you a gift and you turning right around and giving them a gift, *on your birthday!* That's crazy right! So is feeling obligated you must say something back to the person who just gave you the gift of a heartfelt compliment. Instead of returning a knee-jerk, just say thank you and meanwhile let the person who complimented you enjoy their good deed for the day instead of you telling them something you clearly don't mean. If you must give this person a compliment, wait a week then give them a nice heartfelt and thoughtful compliment when they deserve it. But not before, or they'll know it's not true.

Once you have that down pat, make sure you're never the pseudo-smug compliment receiver. This person makes you regret opening your mouth. They act as if everyone should compliment them, and when they finally get one, look at you as if to say, "Well, what took you so long?" This person is almost just as bad, but they make you feel the same way, like you should have never bothered saying anything to them in the first place. When you get a compliment say thank you and wish that person a great day.

Make a habit of looking in the mirror and smiling. Practice makes perfect.

Another fun and quick way to work on your confidence is practicing your smile. I know that this one might make you feel a little weird, but as they say (and as we've covered), practice doesn't make perfect; perfect practice makes perfect. Therefore the more you practice the principles here, the better off they will work for you in the real world.

When you practice your smile, I encourage you to get in front of your bathroom mirror (this is the best time to practice this by the way, because it's just you and the mirror) and smile. Then after you smile a couple of times, rate your own smile. Was it genuine? Warm? Too much teeth? Not enough teeth? Were your eyes involved in the action? As well as a couple other points. But all in all, does it honestly look like you would welcome the same smile you're giving from other people? If the answer is no, then it's back to the drawing (or smiling) board. Feel free to ask your friends, family or significant other with help on this. Because we didn't cover specifically practicing your smile much in the smile chapter, here we are. Remember, if you are having difficulty making that smile realistic, aka genuine, refer back to your Dandelion List. This should brighten you right up, if you've taken the time and really thought that list through. When in doubt, you can never fail by resorting back to the "fake it 'til you make it" philosophy. Force yourself to feel good, take deep breaths. You can do this!

> ### ⊕ Millionaire Mannerism:
> **Perfect practice makes perfect.**

Stick to your personal code.

Another huge part of having genuine confidence and letting it shine through no matter where you are is the comforting feeling that you know what you will do in different situations. One of the toughest things to do in life is anticipating what others will do. Now it is possible with training and in certain types of scenarios to be able to do this, but all in all, it's best to have a strategy worked out for yourself on what you will do if a, b or c take place. Acting with confidence when a question arises is a major tool in the toolbox.

It's been said that your morals and ethics should be the light when there is darkness ahead of you, and I believe that to be true, but first you must define what your personal code is. Some have codes that are very simple while others are very complicated, but the common thread is that they all should provide a gameplan. What you will do and what won't you do in any given circumstance. Imagine the latter part as your own personal line in the sand. Some examples could be you drawing a line in reference to dealing with money, i.e. you will always have a contract in place; or you saying you will only do business with people who have done x, y and z; or that the feelings of your family will trump many other things, i.e. I know several folks whose date nights with their wives will not be sacrificed for anything if they can help it. While these are only a few surface examples, they are meant to help get the juices flowing to help you on the road to creating your own set. A few more suggestions to help:

- Try dividing your code into the same compartments of your life to start. As you list them out, you will inevitably see overlap.
- Study the codes of some of your favorite people, no matter if they are a noteworthy person, celebrity, or your favorite uncle, pick a few people whom you admire, and who you'd like to emulate on some level and look to pick up bits and pieces you can use.
- Ask those closest to you for input regarding what they value; you may be missing something critical.
- Talk to your parents.
- Study the tenets of your Holy Book.

All in all, this personal code means to be comforting and reliable for you, and available to you when situations get rough. When you are stumped and don't know where to turn I recommend your code.

Help as many other people as you can.

One of my favorite ways to recommend folks get an immediate confidence boost is to perform enough good deeds, service and value adding acts that people have no choice but to shower you with thanks. There is no better feeling or boost to one's self-worth than simply hearing the words, "thank you." These two simple words are closely related to the smile. When combined, they are a potent mixture of alchemy that typically will grant the user whatever it is they are desiring. This is because, as Dale Carnegie says in his timeless classic *How to Win Friends and Influence People,* almost every single solitary person you meet, no matter their position, bank account or station in life, has an imaginary sign around their neck that reads, *make me feel important.* Usually when you do a good job of this you will be thanked more often than not, and thanked genuinely to boot. What another wonderful example of a win-win. Your confidence is boosted (and you can also use this method of service delivery to get an inkling of what you were meant to do in this world), and meanwhile you are providing service to those who want, need, and ultimately appreciate what you do.

As far as karmic deposits go, this is as good as it gets, and the cool thing is that you can do it as much as you want to! And the more services you perform in this manner, the more your reputation will grow and precede you in the best way possible. One of my favorite sayings is when you talk about yourself, it's called bragging, but when others talk about you it's called proof. Remember that one of our primary objectives of this entire book is helping you establish your reputation. The more service you provide, the more people will view you as an asset, and the more they will talk about you positively. Then when you combine this reputation with your knowledge of Millionaire Manners, it will be tough for you to lose!

🔍 Millionaire Mannerism:

When you talk about yourself, it's called bragging, but when others talk about you, it's called proof.

Avoid perfectionism.

One of the worst mistakes I see people make with this material, on projects, or life in general is that they wait for every star to be aligned and every traffic light to turn green before they make a move. This is what experts call "analysis paralysis," where you look at things so long and hard that you eventually psyche yourself right out of any action. Another word for this is perfectionism and it is the enemy of greatness. This might sound slightly counterintuitive but allow me to offer up a few examples. When Bill Gates released the very first version of Microsoft Windows do you think it was perfect, or that it had a few kinks? What about the very first iPhone, MacBook, or even the first airplane or car? You think they just rolled off the assembly line perfect or do you think the creators hustled and worked their fingers to the bone to get *something* out to the people and then made changes? You probably already know the answer. They also say it's easier to steer the ship once it's moving, and I offer to you that **you** as the biggest project you've ever worked on are also a work in progress. You matter but you must be patient with yourself. I don't mean make excuses for yourself, but if you are out trying to be better and trying to practice this information and material daily, you are going to mistakes. And I'm here to tell you that it's ok.

I had a mentor once tell me when I was making a decision on whether to do something, or looking to give one of my employees autonomy to make something happen, that as long as it didn't cost money and everyone would remain safe, go for it. This is the best advice I can give you as we move along. Don't be too hard on yourself. Lots of granite gets broken off in the process of creating a masterpiece, and to make an omelet you must break the eggs!

Millionaire Mannerism:

Remember that granite gets broken when you're sculpting a masterpiece!

Millionaire Morals:

- Doing for others is one of the best ways to feel good about yourself and build confidence.
- Practicing what you love is another way.

Action:

1. Practice your smile in the mirror. Today.
2. Write out your personal code on paper and read it. Confidence comes from consistency.
3. Be thankful daily.

PART THREE:
MANNERS

CHAPTER 8

Weddings (from an attendee perspective).

What is the proper attitude to attend a wedding with?

Many times in life we don't approach situations with the proper attitude and perspective, and wonder why they turn out in a less than stellar fashion. It is with this spirit I offer the first piece of advice regarding attending a wedding, and really any event for that matter, and that's if you accept the invitation and decide to attend, attend with the right attitude. What is the right attitude? The right attitude to attend an event should be one of positivity and gratitude. I've seen many people accept invitations begrudgingly, attend, and think that it's ok to tear down this person's event who went out of their way to invite you. This is absolutely incorrect, inappropriate, and almost guarantees that this person will make it a point to attend your next event and tear it down. However, if you see the invitation for what it is, an honorary request to share in what is usually a special occasion for another person, your attitude should reflect this honor you have been bestowed with via their invitation to you. Treat every invitation as an honor and your attitude will be in line.

The last thing to consider about an invitation is that by definition it is a request for your presence, and as is the case with most requests, you have the option to oblige or deny the request. Therefore, because most invitations are optional (except maybe those from your boss, which we'll cover later) think wisely before accepting or rejecting them. I cannot stress enough that if you do accept, don't attend and then be upset when you do and take it out on everyone else in attendance. It's in poor taste. If you don't like the person who invited you all that much, or there isn't a great networking opportunity there, don't go, and be happy with your decision.

Millionaire Mannerism:

Treat every invitation as an honor!

The art of the RSVP (and to really any occasion).

As we laid out in the first section, the foundation to receiving the invitation, gratitude, is the same basis with which you should also respond to the invitation as well. Before you think that RSVP'ing is unnecessary, try planning an event of your own without knowing how many people are actually coming. That's because there's literally only one thing worse than not responding and showing up, and that is to respond in the affirmative then not show! The latter is probably a little worse than the former. It's all about being gracious and being honored, as well as showing respect for the person who invited you into their world. RSVP'ing (or in French to respond s'il vous plaît [if you please]) is a respectful way to acknowledge the request for your presence and politely and respectfully accept or decline. Count on not being invited to many events if you don't respect the RSVP.

There's also the art of knowing which events to attend and which to not attend. As a general rule, invitations from the boss are a good idea to at attend least for a portion of the event. Even if you don't stay the whole time, just by making an attempt to show up could bode well for adding to your reputation as either a team player, or just as someone with good manners, Millionaire Manners even. The other factors to keep in mind are more selfish, but often times you can kill two birds with one stone, and that is to attend a less than appealing event, but look at it as a networking opportunity. Every gathering is an opportunity to connect with those in the same field as you, or those in other fields depending on the nature of the gathering. Either way, making it a point to attend with a good attitude and open mind will usually make the event a lot more bearable and even allow you to have a good time when you may have had a different thought going in.

When you have the chance to, consider leaving an explanation for why you might not be able to attend, and by all means stay away from the wishy-washy, and personally dreaded "maybe." If anything, simply take a little longer to RSVP, but make a decision. It won't be the end of the world if you decline due to a conflict, or a serious desire to not attend. If you really want to attend, make it a priority and get there. If you receive a verbal invitation, don't commit right away either, just let the person know you will check your calendar and get back to them. Then check your calendar and get back to them. Either way, just decide and avoid looking like you have a problem with commitment. Also, a wedding is a big deal so be happy!

⊚ Millionaire Mannerism:

Avoid responding to invitations with a maybe; it makes it look like you have a problem with commitment.

What to wear: two factors (what season and time of day).

Thankfully weddings happen mostly during the spring and summer so the choices of what to wear are somewhat narrowed down for you. You don't have to worry about wearing a coat that could clash with your suit or business casual attire, which is a good thing. It also means you can get away without wearing a tie, because it's usually warm during spring and summer weddings. But alas, the two main factors to help you decide what to wear are season, and time of day. If it's a winter wedding you probably don't want to break out the white linen or khakI cotton suit with pastel tie get up. Those are probably much more fitting selections for spring time nuptials. If you are attending a fall or winter wedding, darker colors are always appropriate. Think plaid suits, heavy material like tweed, wool, or other textured material. If it is a classic spring/summer ceremony, think those lighter materials we mentioned earlier, and lighter colored accents always work well. Feel free to ask either the organizer, or pay attention to the invitation (here it is again) to make sure the host or organizer hasn't requested guests to wear something special. This does happen from time to time.

Overall though, the object is for you to be as comfortable and good looking as possible while honoring the occasion and guests as much as possible. As we've discussed repeatedly it's absolutely possible to have both; again think win-win. Being poorly dressed and making the host feel uncomfortable is not the impression you want to leave on the occasion so make sure you're paying attention. When in doubt though, the light gray suit is usually perfect for all occasions regardless of season. Pair the color of the tie to the season and you'll always be fashionable!

What gift is appropriate?

The real question is, what gift isn't appropriate? I think we all know what this means. Have you personally ever turned down a gift? And aren't you more appreciative of everything as you get older? Remember when it used to be about quantity over quality? To our younger readers, don't worry, you'll know this feeling soon enough. This section of the wedding chapter is somewhat of a gloss over because we delve deeper in a coming chapter on the exact rules of gift-giving, and give you some pretty useful tips to make it happen and become your family's gift-giving ninja.

Wedding gift-giving usually comes down to this simple rule, bring something. Usually a card says a lot, but a card with something inside says even more. It says we're classy and we didn't come empty-handed. It says I value you and your invitation and am happy for you. It also says when you get invited to my next function you won't forget my generosity here today. Of course reciprocity is not why you do it, but simply an added bonus. Ultimately still, you are building your reputation into one of reliability, class and thoughtfulness, and therefore the old adage rings true even for gift-giving: It's truly the thought that counts. There's only one caveat though. That caveat is to always consider your audience, meaning if your host or hostess is more into high-end things, you may want to spring, whereas if their taste is a bit more pedestrian a gift from the home section of your local big-box could work just the same. The moral of the story remains the same: bring something with you and you'll feel better about yourself!

The toast and why it's important (and if you should even give one).

Giving on the fly speeches or toasts for any occasion can be daunting. Being able to give a proper toast and have all the elements and training down pat could be another entire book in and of itself, but again, I'll simply give you an overview and a few pointers to make sure you nail this. You must consider the occasion, how well you know the person, gauge the audience for appropriateness, etc. Having some ammo and know-how never hurt. As a general rule I recommend that everyone reading this book immediately go out and join their local active

Toastmasters International chapter. For those of you who don't know, Toastmasters is an international public speaking club that will help you hone both your speaking skills and leadership, all in a supportive, positive and engaging environment. I have been a member for years, and I can tell you that the experience has been amazing. In short, this is the sort of environment and setting that can help you prepare giving a toast at a wedding, or an impromptu introduction of a good friend at a random event you might find yourself at. Either way, speaking and thinking on your feet is a trainable skill that will pay for itself many times over.

If you know you're going but not sure how the toasts or open mike will go after the ceremony, take the time to write down a few remarks for the bride or the groom. Plan on keeping it G-rated because there could be children or elderly folk in attendance (although elderly folks routinely tell me some of the raunchiest jokes ever). As you're crafting this piece, think of all the ways this person is now lucky to be having so-and-so, but you also want to try to include some piece of personal history between you and whoever your friend in the wedding is. The moral of this brief toast should be to highlight your happiness for the new couple and to be as tasteful and classy as possible. This is a feat for many because public speaking routinely ranks among the largest fears for most Americans, but with preparation you can easily overcome this and make a real impression on everyone in attendance.

Who should I bring to a wedding with me?

Once again I say very carefully to refer back to the wedding invitation. Well done invitations will include all the pertinent details including ones like this. Very rarely will kids be allowed at weddings, but there are exceptions to every rule. Many weddings, no matter how close you may be, only allow invitees to attend by themselves, i.e. no guests. Practices like this one are the exception and not the rule, however you must respect your friend or planner and their rules. The same rules apply when faced with potentially awkward situations, such as when I was once not able to bring my wife to a wedding reception. I remained gracious, and attended with a smile that said I was honored to have been invited.

Multicultural weddings.

One of the best ways to receive a crash course in another culture or religion is to be invited to a multicultural wedding, or have the opportunity to participate in one. Two of the best times I ever had at weddings were the weddings of two different cultures vastly different from my own. One was an affair that had all the styling's and flavor of the Panamanian bride, and the other was a traditional Orthodox Jewish wedding. These were a cultural eye-opener for me for sure, but the one thing they both had in common was the joy, love and happiness that was present at each one. I was happy to have been able to attend, and my attitude showed.

I've been fortunate enough to have attended many weddings and each one of them has had a very different flavor. The other constant at most of the weddings I've attended, unfortunately, is the varying depth of negativity. Yes, believe it or not, as I've alluded to before, there are actually some people who attend these joyous occasions not to celebrate and send cheer and glad tidings but to send bad vibes while commiserating and bemoaning its participants. Make it your business to stay clear away from these people. If you happen to be caught in the cross fire of some negative comments, or in the middle of a group where this type of talk is about to begin, run. If you're trapped, or someone you came with happens to have been the fire starter, do not comment, and if possible try to redirect the conversation to positive or neutral territory. I say this for a couple of reasons. Firstly, you never know who knows who.

I've seen many a normal negative tirade turn even worse for the deliverer once he realizes that one of the people he's talking **to** is related to the person he's talking **about.** Talk about awkward! I'm not saying don't be negative for fear of someone telling someone else you're a negative person, but rather it is a horrible thing to do by spreading negativity at someone else's wedding. The second and more important reason is that you wouldn't want someone doing it to you.

Empathy is a topic we haven't explored too deeply so far, but it is a surprisingly applicable topic as it pertains to manners. We've covered the notion of the classic "Golden Rule" and its updated cousin, but empathy is the underlying and proverbial gold in the conductor's connection between these lessons and applying them to people you come in contact with. Sympathy might say "if that were me," while empathy says "that *is* me." This is a very stark contrast to what we might think. Many say, and I agree, that empathy could transform the way many of us treat one another overnight. Empathy breeds thoughtful conduct, while sympathy breeds sorrow, and contempt breeds arrogance. Make it a practice to put yourself not in the other person's shoes, but in that person's whole body.

How to handle parents' weddings (remarried?).

Your parents no matter their age want nothing more than for you to love their new mate as much as they do, or as much as you love them. In reality it rarely happens but it should do nothing to stop your whole-hearted attempt. It should most certainly not deter you from approaching the entire endeavor with the proper attitude and perspective. The perspective I mention is the exact same one that will permeate your own circumstance when it comes time for you to marry or remarry. This should be the group of people we unconditionally support, especially in our families as long as the objective is to improve one's life. These sorts of situations almost always require our positive attention and support in order for them to turn out in the best way possible. Therefore offer up your support, love and service when presented with the opportunity to do so. You can then become the go-to person, or "point" person for those who may even have doubts on the union. It is your unwavering positivity, love and support that can unwittingly, and maybe even desirably, cast you into the role of de facto leader. How cool is that? It's also great practice for putting aside personal feelings, like you may have to do in a work setting, for the benefit of the larger team, or in this case, family at large.

It is with this same attitude and premise that you would then go about meeting the family of your parent's new partner. This is something I've personally experienced and a time that can be filled with great apprehension, anxiety and even awkwardness. The best way I've found to approach these types of situations is to not only focus on minding my own attitude but to engage my new family in dialogue around our similarities, not differences. People will usually rally passionately around those things they are interested in, and one sure-fire way to get someone interested in you is for you to be interested in what they are and then talk about it. You will discover a whole new side of people you thought you knew well. We will get into this subject a lot more deeply in subsequent chapter on the art of the conversation, but for the time being, focusing on similarities is always an effective strategy. A quick example is:

Good Similarity Find

Person A: "So where are you originally from?"

Person B: "New York City."

Person A: "Ok nice, I've visited there several times and it's somewhat similar to DC, where I'm from."

Person B: "Exactly, I've heard it gets really cold there too."

You see how the dialogue has both people talking about something near and dear to them?

Not so Good Similarity Find

Person A: "So where are you originally from?"

Person B: "New York City."

Person A: "Well, I've visited there several times and it's nothing like DC, where I'm from."

Person B: "Well I've heard people in DC are pretty rude too."

And there's the end of that conversation. Neither of the people found any common ground with the other. We will explore this topic later in more depth. However the lesson and moral of this section remains the same: Approach your new side of the family with love and respect, keeping in mind your parent wants your love and support on this more than you can ever imagine, and to focus on the similarities when you meet your new family, or anyone new for that matter.

Millionaire Mannerism:

When meeting anyone new, always focus the conversation more on similarities than differences.

How to small talk during the reception.

Small talk during the reception is very similar in nature to what we've discussed previously, with one exception: You don't have the pressure to engage anyone at the reception that is not a part of your new family, but you already knew that. Here's why: As we've spoken about in previous sections and chapters, networking is one of the keys to a successful life. Many have heard the saying that "your network equals your net worth."

I am here to tell you this is absolutely the case. The thing is you can add people to your network literally anywhere and anytime by keeping your eyes and ears open and taking advantage of situations where you run into new people. A wedding reception, therefore, is an excellent place to start.

Controversial topics, however, are never the place to start. As we get into more depth of how to start a conversation or what to do when your existing conversation begins to wane, this is one notion to keep in mind. You have to keep in mind why people consider certain topics to be taboo, off-limits, or controversial. It's usually because they may share an opinion of the view that might not be that popular among the masses, or one that elicits such an emotional and visceral response that they don't like talking about it with people they do not know. When topics that fit into this category are raised, those with certain views may simply withdraw altogether from the conversation, and you may have lost this person permanently. Now if someone else brings up one of these such topics and you are able to engage in a non-emotional way (which is very tough) then by all means join in, but make sure you are aware of your own emotions, because if not, it could end badly for you.

Another cool way to handle receptions with those you don't really know is to play the "who do you know and how do you know them" game. This is a fun way to explore the type of relationship that all these people in the room may have with those being honored. It's also a cool and fun way to learn some interesting facts about your friend that even you might not be privy to. But don't pry! Just ask a few questions to get things going, then go with the flow. No need to be creepy!

What should you do and not do at a wedding reception?

"Life of the party" is a term we here all the time in relation to that person who always seems to have fun wherever he or she is, and to the trained eye doesn't really look like he's faking it either. This is because this person is comfortable with who he is, has confidence, and probably had something to drink already! But seriously, this is usually a person who is enjoying the company of everyone at the function, or at least as many people as he can, and is enjoying it as it happens. But what the "life of the party" really means is that this person isn't waiting for someone to give them an invitation before loosening up a bit and engaging those around him to do the same. Take for instance if you're a dinner party, why not suggest a couple games for the group to play? Or if you're at this same party, why not suggest a change in music to get things a bit more lively? These are just a couple suggestions from "the life of the party manual."

Another key thing at a wedding, dinner party, or anywhere there's music, lose the too cool for school act and grab your woman and hit the dance floor! There's no other more sure-fire way to get things going at a function than to be the first to get on the dance floor. I'm not talking ballroom quality either per se, just get out there and stick to the basics of what you know, and you will undoubtedly be crowned the life of the party for this singular act alone.

The good guest's pledge!

All in all, the rules of this chapter can be summed up in a simple way: Don't ruin someone else's function because you're having a bad day. Read over this good guest pledge and make the pledge before attending your next wedding or any other function where someone else honored you with an invitation, and where your own reputation is on line (which is every time)!

During the Ceremony

- I will respect the sanctity of the occasion and not talk during the wedding ceremony or interrupt the service by taking pictures with a flash camera. This is also not the time to mingle or loudly greet friends or acquaintances. I will turn off the ringers on my cell phone and pager.

- I will participate in as much of the ceremony as my own religion and that of the ceremony permit. If a mass or communion is offered and I choose not to participate, I will remain quietly in my seat. Otherwise, I'll stand when others stand and sit when others sit. I am not required to kneel or to recite prayers that are contrary to my own beliefs.
- I will not show up at the ceremony or reception with a surprise guest, whether a date, children, or extras in general.

During the Reception

- I will not grab the microphone to croon a few favorite numbers, no matter how impressive my singing voice, or broadcast stories or jokes, no matter how humorous I think I am.
- I won't monopolize the bride and groom in the receiving line. I will offer brief comments and then move on quickly.
- I will not alter place cards or switch tables at the reception. Instead, I will be as cordial as I can be wherever the bride and groom have designated that I sit. I will introduce myself to my tablemates and add a little explanation about how I know the couple.

After the Reception

- I will not take the centerpiece upon departing, scoop up matchbooks, or request that any uneaten portion of my meal be put in a doggie bag to be taken home.

- I will not get behind the wheel if I've had too much to drink, nor will I allow others who are intoxicated to endanger themselves.

Millionaire Morals:

- You being invited is an honor; behave as such!
- RSVP'ing is the respectful thing to do.
- Behave as if you will see this people again.

Action:

1. Read the fine print of every invitation.
2. Reread the good guest's pledge and promise yourself!

CHAPTER 9

I don't know them that well, should I bring a gift? The Art of Gifting.

Why do people think their gift has to be expensive?

Perceptions are very interesting things in the sense that often they make us do rational and irrational things. As we explore the nature of gift-giving I see one common misconception always creep up, and that is that people are mostly under the impression that if they don't spend a lot of money on a gift, it is somehow insufficient altogether. This couldn't be further from the truth. The majority of people who attend gift-worthy functions do not bring gifts, even though it would be well inside social norms to do so. For these people who bring nothing, and for those who do bring something and still feel self-conscious about it, both sets of people are driven by the misconception that money spent equals love felt. I see it time and time again that instead of focusing on what the person might really like to do, or what fun activities you can participate in with your kids at their birthday party, we spend the time looking for the perfect gift.

The funny thing is perfect gifts do exist, in that it is perfectly selected for its recipient by you. However, there are literally millions of options for what this person would and could end up loving if we simply make a decision. The other interesting fact is that this "money equals love" equation is derivative of us as people sometimes feeling inadequate personally, and therefore looking to make up the difference with green. This is never a good approach. Instead, think of what you love about that person, then lead with that. If you love the way they cook, get them a cookbook. If you love their clothing choices and how they wear a color, get them a nice neck scarf. Whatever you do, don't confuse money with caring or love; this is the opposite of the definition of a gift, which is something given willingly to someone without payment or expectation of repayment. The old adage is absolutely applicable here with respect to gift-giving, and that is: it's the thought that counts.

🖲 Millionaire Mannerism:

When choosing a gift, it really is the thought that counts, so put some thought into it!

What are the three foolproof gifts everyone should know?

As we stated in the previous section, let it be known once more there is no such thing as the perfect gift, only one that you perfectly select, with thought, for that special person. Ironically, it's usually the presence of a large sum of money spent on a gift that means the absence of thought. This is because usually the person receiving an expensive gift is operating under the same false pretense of money equaling love, so they happily accept it. Of course this portion isn't meant to say at all that expensive gifts can't be thoughtful, but more often than not, it takes more than money alone to give a great and thoughtful gift.

There are a couple of go-to gifts that almost never get old, and that you always have access to if you run out of time.

1. **Flowers**. We've spoken about these before but these never gets old (even though the flowers do!). You can get them for your wife, girlfriend, or your mother and get the same loving and happy reaction every time. You can give them to men and women, for birthdays or funerals, and again get the same thankful smile in return. You can never lose by giving flowers.

2. **A gift certificate to your favorite spa or massage parlor**. This is another gender-neutral gift that almost everyone loves. Luckily we live in one of the most self-indulgent times in history this side of the Ancient Greeks, so we love ourselves more than ever. That being said, everyone loves one more opportunity to pamper themselves, and pampering yourself on someone else's dime makes the experience all the better, believe me.

3. **A greeting card with a heartfelt, handwritten message**. It's easy to get a greeting card nowadays. You can pick them up from your local convenience store, drug store or big-box retailer, but they need one thing to make them special, and that's your handwritten sentiment. Many times people will get a card for someone and ignore the massive amount of open space inside each card. That space isn't there just to look empty, it's there so you can script out your personal thoughts to the person receiving the card. Not that the poem inside doesn't speak volumes, but your personal words mean so much more. And if you're feeling up to it, slide a $20 inside and you'll always be thought highly of.

What should I get for a kid?

One of my pet peeves has always been those parents whose child is invited to a birthday party, but they allow their own children to attend empty-handed! That your child was invited in the first place is a sign of respect, but to show up without anything in hand shows a lack of appreciation for being invited. In the last section I detailed several quick items you can always bring. It's even easier to shop for kids. Here's a quick overview: Kids love toys, sweets and money! With this trifecta alone you should never be forced to send your kid to a party empty-handed. Think of the adult version of this scene. Person is invited to party, they eat up all the host's good food and drink, have a good time, but never think to pay their share. No one is ever going to mention this to you, they'll just simply file it away after doing the math on who brought something and who didn't. Then the word will spread. Don't let it!

What I like to do is keep a couple of toys on hand in the house for a variety of reasons. First off, kids of the same age mostly enjoy the same type of toys. If we ever need something, I grab it from the stash. If nothing is coming up anytime soon, I like to give them out randomly to my son for a job well done, as I catch him doing something good. We've talked about being honored and appreciative for every invitation received, and training our children on this same philosophy can never start too early. Show respect to get respect, and taking a gift is always a good first step.

What should I give for wedding gifts?

Practical gifts for a wedding are my absolute gift of choice. This is because anyone who has ever been married knows that when uniting in spirit, you are also uniting and joining households, and probably in a new space. Therefore the more useful a gift you give the better. Weddings are just about the only time I'll go against one of my own self-imposed standards of never giving gift cards. This is because as you unite two households, this means uniting toasters, microwaves, and dishes. To go and add to this mess won't exactly get you any cool points with the new couple. Therefore go ahead and write a nice note in the card, bring some flowers, and then drop a gift card or even cash in the envelope. They get to keep the card as a nice memory and won't curse you every time they go to use their third microwave.

I'll repeat one other aspect of attending weddings and how to give gifts as well though, and that is to never go empty-handed. I know I've mentioned this part several times already so forgive the redundancy, but there are few things more classless and thoughtless than this. Time management is something we won't get all the way into in this book, but as humans we always, and I mean always, make time for what we want to do. This is the first rule of time management. Whatever you are endeavoring to complete must be worth your time or you will never do it well. Gift-giving is no different. A little effort goes a long way and the recipient will be able to tell every single time.

What is appropriate for birthday gifts?

Fun is on top of the mind for every single youth in America. Therefore your primary target when selecting a gift for a young person is can they can fun with it? If the answer is no, then immediately go back to square one and reevaluate your gift. I don't want this to sound like rocket science, but think back hard to when you were eight or ten and that Aunt of yours, who you loved dearly, bought you a book. Yep, she bought you a book while all your friends were getting Transformers and Batman action figures. Save yourself a reenactment of this when buying a gift for the friend of your kid, or just make sure you're the hero at the party for your little cousin or nephew and not getting the half-hearted "I don't want to look sad and embarrass you" smile at gift opening time.

I'll also tell you that you don't have to spend nearly as much thought time as you would have to do when shopping for your mother or significant other, but take your time and don't be careless with your decision. Children have excellent memories and we want all the children in our lives to have childhoods that are filled with as many great memories as possible, and here's your chance to be on the good side of one. Many times we get upset with children for wanting to be children at the wrong times instead of facilitating time when they can just run amuck without fear of punishment or rules. Let's make sure our gifts allow them to do just that.

How does gift-giving separate you?

Class is something that a lot of people think can be bought like any other common commodity you might purchase at the grocery store. The people who have thoughts like this are, unfortunately, among the most classless walking around. This is because there is a certain group of individuals who equate money to all things, and do not realize that the best things in life are earned or learned yet never purchased. One of the top primary objectives of this entire book is to separate yourself from the "classless masses" around us and create a sort of "manners vortex" that will pull in all casual observers, admirers, and common folk to you so that they will have no other course of action but to ask you to teach them all you know. This is the desire of this book in general, and gift-giving is one of the key ingredients to this cause.

Thoughtfulness in general is one of the most fleeting characteristics in existence today. This is attributable to the fact that most of the time people are expecting something in return for their acts of kindness, while the Millionaire Manners Ambassador understands that the only way to gain is to give it all away, and expect nothing in return. This is thoughtfulness and selflessness all the way. As you do these types of things, gift away your precious belongings or bestow your favorite items onto others, you will inspire others to do the same. This is the movement that changes everything!

The perfect gift for grandparents for any occasion.

Now back to more tips that will ensure you become, and remain the gift-giving ninja you can be. Grandparents as a general rule are some of the sweetest human beings to walk the planet. This is because they've mostly lived full lives, and in the twilight of their life have an abundance of time to shower us with copious amounts of love and affection. Therefore they make prime targets for random acts of gift-giving to partially pay them back for the years of birthday checks in the amount of the year you were born (don't tell me I'm the only one who got these!). At this point in their lives, a Grandparent's main currency is memories. The more they get from you and/or know how they helped form your own, the better. This is how I realized many years ago that my grandparents and yours absolutely love receiving anything handwritten from you. It could be for a birthday, a holiday, or just an "I was thinking of you" card, and they will love it. They will love it because it took you time to write it, and this is the one resource that when it's gone, it's gone.

The other really cool side effect of writing handwritten notes to your mother or grandparents is that you get to practice the other increasingly doomed dark art of cursive penmanship. This is one of those skills that is no longer being taught in schools and therefore will be super valuable in the future. At the least you will be able to wow all your younger family members at some point in time. The moral here is anytime you can show someone you put effort into what you did for them, they will love you for it and appreciate it even more.

What kinds of gifts should you focus on?

As we conclude this chapter I want to prove a point just so you know I haven't been pulling your leg this entire time I've been describing all these "perfect" gifts. I want you to take a moment and think back to every perfect gift you've ever received in your life. Didn't they seem to speak directly to you? Wasn't it yours because someone was listening when you didn't even mean for them to be? Wasn't it something that made you smile, and you could have fun with and be yourself with? I ask you to reflect on these because these are the types of reactions you want from those you give gifts to. You almost want to be seen as psychic! But mostly you want to lead this mission from your heart, and ensure you are looking for thought-filled and heart-filled items to pass onto to your friends and loved ones.

Remember that it doesn't have to be expensive in order for you to win at this game. Don't be cheap, but don't think a hefty price tag equals a great gift. Lastly I want you to consider what type of memories you are hoping this person will create with what you are giving them. Will they be happy and fun memories, or will they be forgettable memories? The choice rests solely with you!

Millionaire Morals:

- Thoughtful gifting is done from the heart.
- Put thought into your choice; don't worry about cost, or lack thereof.

Action:

1. NEVER go empty-handed!
2. Remember the three fail-safe gifts: flowers, massage certificates, and greeting cards with handwritten messages.

CHAPTER 10

I don't know them that well, should I leave a tip? The Art of Tipping.

What is the history of tipping?

We can thank England for many things, such as the colors of our flag, the inspiration to start a revolution, and rugby. In addition to these wonderful contributions to life in the West, we can thank our former countrymen for the phenomenon of tipping. Many historians trace this once odd practice of paying for what should be expected to eighteenth century England where urns used to be placed on counters in pubs with the words "to insure promptitude" across them. Promptitude, of course, is a fancy English word for great service. It was so pervasive in the olden days that it really did increase your chances for great service by leaving a tip. From these pubs spread the practice of giving money to servants for better service all over Europe. But when these same visitors went to other parts of the world, including America, they were astonished to see that coachmen, porters and waiters thought of themselves as employees and thus would not accept tips from travelers. Tipping slowly became accepted in America, and by the 1910s about five million workers had tip-taking jobs. Fast forward to 2003 and *reported* tips from American restaurants alone reached nearly $26 Billion!

Why do I begin with giving you a history of tipping? It's to make sure you have an accurate portrayal of how this and other practices came to be, but also to ensure empathy is always on the top of your mind. The Millionaire Manners Ambassador in you should always want to know why a practice or particular ritual is going on, and not feel obligated one way or another except to do what is right, not what is expected. This is just one more opportunity to lead by example and encourage those around you to ask questions before they participate.

Don't tip because of this.

Expectations alone should never be enough to make anyone do anything. There should be thought and a combination of factors before we act. This is the case as it pertains to tipping. I tell people all the time that pressure to tip should never make you tip. You should also never tip just because there is a line that says you should. Tips should only be given when service expectations are at a minimum level. For minimum level service, minimum level tips should be left. For excellent and exemplary service, excellent tips should be left. As someone who believes in taking care of people who take care of me, I never tip just because. Those in this industry should earn it or get out of this line of work.

This is no time or reason to be rude or callous though, just don't feel pressured into tipping is all I maintain. Service is key, and that alone should be your standard. The other interesting thing to consider about tipping is that it is always given after the service is completed. Have you ever paid for a haircut beforehand? Have you ever tipped the guy before your car is finished at the wash? The answer is probably no because the job isn't complete until you sign off and okay it. Lastly, tips can be used as a goodwill generator if you plan on returning to a certain place. This is even where meeting some of the staff combined with good tips can ensure you are always taken care of, even when everyone else is waiting for hours.

How/When to address poor service at a restaurant.

Feedback is one of the tips and gifts of the truly generous and self-aware. I say this because without it, how would you know half of what you do now? Trial and error is one thing but telling someone up front, without prejudice or emotion is how people around you grow and get better. Restaurant workers are no different. If you've received horrible service and are dissatisfied with your meal, the best way to make a stand is to request to speak to the restaurant owner. As a business owner there is no one who cares more passionately about the quality and service in the place you just ate more than the owner. Especially if he didn't just buy the restaurant from someone else. Therefore true power lies in telling the person with the power and motivation to do something about it. Think about this as well, how many folks do you know who experience poor service care enough to actually tell someone about it? That means by the time you reach the owner or manager they will respect your opinion even more because they know that most people just leave.

⊙ Millionaire Mannerism:

Feedback is the gift of the generous and truly self-aware among us.

If the owner is not available then make it a point to speak to the restaurant manager, whom most likely will be available in the owner's absence. You'll get some results, just not as much as you would in speaking to the owner. I tell people all the time that sometimes people do the right things for the wrong reasons, and giving feedback in a restaurant is sometimes put in this category. I bring this up because one more bit of motivation for you could be the fact you'll probably be rewarded with some sort of gift to encourage your return, but this shouldn't be your only motivation. That should be to improve the experience and showcase your generosity to the staff at the restaurant. And for great effect, if it has been really bad, before you pay the bill ask the waiter to go and grab the manager for you. This is where it gets good, because after ignoring you all evening your waitperson will suddenly become all ears and super attentive, and inevitably ask, "Is there something I can help you with?" At this point you should tell them exactly what you're about to tell their boss. They will then think twice the next time around.

Believe me, this is far more effective than just leaving a $1 tip. The waiter won't get the message, they'll just think you're cheap. Don't leave nothing either, they'll think you're dumb and simply forgot. If you want real change speak to someone with the power to change it.

Last rule; make sure that you compliment as easily as you criticize. This takes even more effort because normally our expectations should have been to have a great time. So when great service does happen we are not always impressed. Complimenting the owner/manager or even chef leaves a lasting impression.

🖥 Millionaire Mannerism:

Make sure you compliment as easily as you criticize.

Airports.

Here's a special tip for those readers who travel a good amount. If you are like most travelers I know, it means you have missed a good amount of flights for one reason or another, not unrelated to your own slowness perhaps? A quick remedy is to tip yourself right through the lines. I'm not talking about handing out $5s or even $10s, just make sure you have at least $10 in one dollar bills that you can hand out to everyone who you come across. When I'm telling you people remember this and will want to take care of you, it's no understatement, especially if you travel a lot. Remember, the people who work at the airport work there all the time. So if you haven't been late or missed a flight lately, you will, and then this lesson will become extra useful.

When in a hurry don't panic, just reach in your pocket and use those dollars to grease the wheels of industry and watch things happen. This sort of special treatment is usually reserved for dignitaries and celebrities, but you can share in their power by helping to create special memories for the workers at the airport. This is because there is a strong emotional connection to money. This is why tipping, especially in cash is so powerful. I don't know about you, but I still get excited finding even a quarter on the ground! Imagine if you didn't expect a tip and someone just up and hands you a dollar or two? You'll likely not forget this person any time soon. Herein lies the great power of tipping when you don't have to.

Barbershops

The way I operate in a barbershop is a little different, only because I expect to return if I like the haircut, the service was good, and the shop is at least presentable. This is because I've come across some really run down shops where the barbers and service were really good. Therefore, when establishing a relationship with a new barber it helps to not tip the first time around. This is because he may or may not know exactly what you like, and you haven't figured out his style yet either. That's why I always reserve the tip for the second haircut and so on. It takes us back to the very first lesson of tipping, and that is to never tip just because someone else expects us to. We're much better off explaining to the person what we like (feedback) so they can nail it the next time.

That's why it's also important to be very specific with a new barber so he knows exactly what you want, so that he can eventually earn a tip from you, and also to ensure he doesn't flat-out destroy your head! We'll revisit the topic of giving specific and detailed instructions in another chapter or book, but there's nowhere it's more applicable than in a barbershop. Tipping also ensures you will leave a memorable impression on your barber, and not have to wait as long, and that he even wants to continue cutting your hair. A common misconception is that barbers can't control or choose their clients. This is completely false, and hopefully there is a barber reading this right now who will either agree, or in who a light bulb just went off. If a client is a problem, fire them. If your barber is a problem fire him!

How to ask for information?

Travelling can be one of the scariest times in life. Therefore you should never hesitate to ask for help when out and about. What you should be more aware of is how to do it properly. As it stands now, many people around the world view Americans as greedy, arrogant people. Unfortunately, some of these stereotypes are reinforced when we travel abroad, and thus become true in the minds of the locals. Do us all a favor and work to reverse some of these views by exercising humility when asking for anything, and not just in a foreign land. Many times people ask questions of strangers as if that person owes them something, like correct information. They do not. Exercise that empathy muscle and ask yourself how you feel when approached by an arrogant foreigner who just as soon asks you a question as easily and readily as they spit on you, and how your answer might look to this individual. Chances are, you're doing your best to make sure they end up not only far away from their destination, but most likely in the bad part of town!

This can be easily addressed though, ensuring you approach strangers with the proper humility and respect because you need them, not the other way around. Combine this attitude with a well-placed tip and you'll be well on your way to unlocking secrets you didn't know existed in either your own town, or wherever else you find yourself. Then you will also set yourself up for one of the coolest things ever to happen to you, and that's when you encounter a perfect storm of you, the humble and possibly wary traveler who's a practitioner of Millionaire Manners, encountering the all-wise native who has studied this art as well, truly hitting it off. When you go to tip them for their time, they're almost offended because you've built such a rapport they only want to help. This is the power of great manners.

Are you a server or in the service industry? How to receive better tips.

Now that we've gone through the tipping experience solely from the perspective of the tip giver, let's take a quick look at what it means to be on the receiving end of a tip. Research has shown there's a couple things you can incorporate right away that allow you to receive better tips. But before we get into those, remember that people are just a mirror of you. Whatever you give out, is exactly what you will get in return, ninety-nine percent of the time. Have a great attitude with your server and you will magically become their favorite customer of the day, and it will show. If you're having a bad day then take it out on your server, count on you having to speak with the owner, when it all could've been avoided by checking your attitude. Now, to the tips. Remember you can apply these almost anywhere, anytime, no matter if you work in the service industry or not.

a. Always give your name. This seems like rule number one right? Wrong. I still go into restaurants where this step is forgotten or ignored and I immediately have a problem.

My other pet peeve is when the name is said, but they really don't care if you heard it or not. This is the same as not saying it all. Say your name so your customers can hear you.

b. Squat next to the table. This subtle move really shows attentiveness to your diners, and shows that you want to make sure you get everything right. People really appreciate effort, even when the results aren't perfect.

c. Touch the customer (when appropriate). I don't mean reach for a hug, but a gentle tap on the shoulder or touch on the arm of the opposite sex shows a humanness and gentleness that most people appreciate. It makes you human to them.

d. Give your diners after-dinner mints. Even if your restaurant doesn't actually provide them, this is something you could either suggest or just do for your customers. You will immediately stand out.

e. Say please, thank you, and my pleasure throughout the evening. Make sure these are in your vocabulary, it will make all the difference.

f. Write the words "thank you" on the receipt for your customer. And of course, whatever you do, make this the hardest you work all night, but never leave a party waiting who is ready to pay. Think of your tip shrinking with every additional minute they wait. Get the check quick, pick it up quick and leave a cute note. You'll be handsomely rewarded.

A quick guide to tipping for certain services.

So to aid with all the info we've covered, and to add in some that we haven't, here's a quick chart to help you remember. This is just a guide so feel free to leave more (or less) depending on the service you receive. Remember, feedback is key to making sure you're not the victim of poor service in the same place more than once. I also know we haven't really addressed the psychological hurdle associated with tipping, and that's to say I know many people feel like tipping is unnecessary and that if those in the service industry wants to make more money, they shouldn't be working in the service industry. This is all well and good, but the reality is that these are the only jobs some people can get, and there are millions who do it, and do it proudly and with great attitudes as they work toward something better. Therefore don't be judgmental, just give what you can, and plan on spending a little more if you're wowed by the service.

Lastly, you get out what you put in so remember; your servers are people too!

Service	Suggested Tip
Barber	15% or minimum of $1
Cabbie	15% of fare
Cabbie + help with bags	$1/bag or $2 if heavy
Large home delivery	$5-$10 or depending on value of item
Gas station attendant for gas pumping	$1-2
Gas station attendant for wiping glass	$2-5, less if you had to ask
Waitperson at restaurant	15-20% of bill, more for exemplary service or larger group
Waitperson at buffet	5-10% depending on what they did
Flower delivery	$4-5
Pizza or home/office food delivery	10-15%

Service	Suggested Tip
Parking lot attendant	$1 unless he gives your car special attention.
Bartender	10-15% of bill
Wedding musicians	$5-10/person
Good DJs	$50-100, more if requests are taken

Millionaire Morals:

- Never give a tip out of obligation.
- Giving feedback is the only real way to improve service.

Action:

1. The next time you have an issue while out, ask to speak to the owner or manager. It works.
2. Check your own attitude before going out; you might be the problem!

CHAPTER 11

Millionaire Manners in the Workplace (Ninety percent of these rules apply to the school setting too).

How should you approach your job for maximum results?

Reputation is the main commodity that nearly all the lessons in this book so far have been intent on building up for you, along with tips to do it better and easier. Now we are moving into the realm of even more practical application. You should feel yourself becoming more and more powerful and confident about meeting the challenges ahead and making sure you're prepared for those you can't see coming yet. This chapter and subsequent sections will ensure you have the foundation for getting more technical into how to win and win regularly.

What should you do to get maximum results at your job? Start with this simple thought and transform it into a habit: Always find a way to do more than you are paid to do. It sounds simple, and that's because it, along with almost everything else in this book is. That's exactly why most people can't seem to fathom that their lives would be completely different by simply doing a bunch of simple things over and over. As you develop this habit, you will also feel yourself getting closer and closer to your goals, and thus closer to becoming a success.

The other key component to being able to do more is to find the value in it, which means you must continue to control your attitude and become the master of it. Without it, these principles will never work for you. Then simply look for opportunities to practice this habit. It could be in the form of turning your assignments in before they are due, or knocking out extra things. Something else to add on is completing an assignment and then making it a point to ask your supervisor what else needs to be done. I assure you, no one has ever asked this question before, and so you will immediately be in rarified space. Enjoy it for a moment then get back to work.

Two simple rules for dressing in the workplace.

One of the best things about writing this book is that I hope I'm giving you insight into certain things you have never heard before, or some that you may have heard but didn't really know if they were true and/or worked. Hopefully you're getting a bit of both. This is how I felt when I first discovered these rules about dressing in the workplace. Here they are:

- If you want to eventually have your boss's job, no matter what it is, then dress like him or a little better. If he wears khakis, then you should only wear khakis and sometimes slacks. If he wears button ups and no polo shirts, then you should never wear polo shirts and sometimes add a tie. If he participates in that dreaded workplace transgression called "Casual Friday," *aka* "Casualty Friday," then make sure you swear it off.
- If you aspire to rise to at least two levels above where you are currently, then take note of how your boss's boss dresses and use them as your example.

No matter which of these you choose, the moral of the story is to always dress as well or better than your supervisor, and never participate in Casualty Friday. Just because you can do something doesn't mean you should. The other suggestion for workplace attire is to carefully observe how certain people dress and where they are in the organization. This is not necessarily a strong and steadfast rule of thumb, but I'm willing to bet that you will see more correlation than you would have thought. This falls into the category of unspoken rules, of which every workplace has many. Try your best to observe as many of them as possible, while validating what you read here and what others have told you too.

How to handle conflict in the workplace.

One of the most heated topics discussed during our Millionaire Manners course is the section on how to handle those workplace conflicts that are inevitable. We all either have or have had in the past a workplace nemesis. That person was the most obnoxious person walking the Earth to us, and we couldn't wait until they were no longer around. The first thing is to make sure that person isn't you very often. Next make sure you observe a few simple guidelines to address and eventually neutralize this productivity draining issue.

First off, never ever backbite this person. We've discussed this topic briefly in other sections, so we are all familiar with the potential backlash that can come from you talking badly about someone's family or friends. Now take away the random element and make it so you will now see these people every day, and the stakes just got a lot higher as to why you do not want to make a habit of this. This makes you look petty and it internally has you stooping to a much lower level, and that is not good for your psyche. Especially when you know what you are trying to become. Resist the urge to engage in back and forths and tit for tats. Everyone loses in this scenario, especially you because you have bigger plans.

Next, confront this person or the issue head on. What I have learned is that unfortunately, people do not expect straightforwardness and honesty. They expect you to simply avoid them as they avoid you, yet neither of you has any idea or recollection how the bad blood began, and most people will let it fester forever. Take control of the situation and ask this person to have coffee with you at lunch, and begin with this line "I've noticed there is some awkwardness (you can insert tension, bad blood or any other synonym) between us, and I wanted us to be able to address this as adults." Make sure you never say they did so-and-so because you will immediately have them on the defense. Then continue with "I'd really like to resolve it." And when they say, like most unaccountable people will unfortunately, "I don't have a problem with you," simply reply, "I didn't think you did, but I'd still like to apologize to make sure we're good." The unexpected or unsolicited apology is one of the most powerful tools the Millionaire Manners Ambassador possesses. The case is closed and sealed with this one move. And here's the thing. Even if they still don't like you, ninety-nine percent of the time this will resolve any issue because you will have earned their respect and caused them to look in the mirror. It is very powerful.

Two more things. You can use this technique with your supervisor or spouse, or neighbor or recreational league teammate. Not everyone likes to initiate straightforwardness, but again, almost everyone respects it. The last step is that if this has been a coworker, just shoot a quick email to your mutual supervisor about how you took the lead and invited so-and-so out for coffee to resolve any differences and boom, you're your boss's favorite again, and you've covered yourself in case this person was the one percent. Not a bad place to be!

How to manage your boss (even one who may not be very good).

The number one thing to consider in this scenario is that one day you'll be a brand new manager too, so go easy on this person. Even if they're not very good, or maybe shouldn't even be in this position is no concern of yours. Your main job is to make your boss's job as easy and smooth as possible. This may seem a little counterintuitive because you might be thinking that the sooner he's out of there, the sooner you'll be promoted right? Wrong! The universe has never and won't ever work this way. You're rewarded when you do things the right way and with the right intentions, so sabotaging your boss or pushing them when they're on the edge is not the way to go.

You want to first present yourself as a resource to your boss, not an adversary. You want to position yourself as a help and not a hindrance. As you will quickly observe, there are many perks that come from being helpful and not a "pain in the you-know-what" for your supervisor. This philosophy is also directly connected to doing more than you are asked and paid to do. Because the more of a resource you can become for your boss, the better. Let's just say he or she start out horribly then all of a sudden get the picture a lot sooner than everyone expected (because they were probably promoted for a reason, mind you) and now it looks like they'll be your boss for a little while longer. Don't you think they will remember who helped them when they struggled? There's no guarantee either way, but I'm willing to bet you'd rather be on one side than the other.

How to manage your team.

I love coaching new managers on how to run their teams and establish discipline and credibility, which go hand in hand.

But, as is the case with the lessons in this book, there are some basic rules with which once you familiarize yourself, you will be so much better that people will wonder where you received all your cool training. Just tell them Millionaire Manners Academy. More than anything, you must realize that there is a right way to do things, a wrong way, and our way. I'll let you guess which one you should choose.

Here's a quick overview on management that I cannot claim credit for, but a philosophy that is tried and true, and also one that I can quantifiably say contributed to some of my early success. The philosophy is in the book *The One Minute Manager* by Drs. Ken Blanchard and Spencer Johnson. In their book they unlock the simple keys to effective management at any level. The remarkable thing about this book is that it can literally be used by teachers, leaders of nonprofits, low-level managers, middle managers and CEOs alike. You can use it too. Here's the synopsis.

One minute goal setting. This is as easy as it sounds. The first thing any employee needs is goals. What exactly are they working on and when is it due to be complete. Goals and timelines are the lifeblood of any organization, no matter what its overall mission. Every task must be broken down enough to know when it's on track and when it's off course. Only then can you start winning. Begin with your team by helping them set short, mid and long-term goals. Then establish set check-ins to monitor.

One minute praising. If you ask people working today what their biggest gripe on the job is, what do you think the majority of them would say? Money? Lack of opportunity? The commute? Nope, the biggest issue for most people is that they don't get enough credit or praise for the job they do. Crazy right? Remember earlier I told you that everyone is walking around with an invisible sign around their neck that says "make me feel important." One minute praising in the workplace is what compliments are in any other setting. Simply tell your people how good of a job they're doing, and they'll do it even harder. The mission is to constantly catch people doing something right instead of conventional wisdom saying catch them doing something bad.

One minute reprimanding. This is simply regular feedback. If someone is doing something wrong or in a way you don't like, tell them. This is the only way it will improve; not by you wishing or via telepathy. Simply tell them what it is and everything else will (mostly) work itself out.

Respect other people's time.

Some people absolutely love to hear themselves talk. This is why some meetings last forever. This is because they are run by people who aren't really interested much in what others have to say. They just want you to "download" what they have to say as they hold court. Rule number one, make sure this isn't you. Next make sure you practice always saying less than what you initially have on your mind. This is good practice for making sure you have fully thought out what you are going to say instead of just blurting out something potentially insensitive or inappropriate that may have the opposite intended effect on your audience. By saying less than is necessary it also causes people to value what you have to say even more. When they know you've carefully considered your contribution before giving it, it tends to be weighted more heavily, and you will command more of an audience as well, as your reputation (there it is again) grows as an insightful person.

Not everyone, but many people who talk and talk and are self-unaware of this issue are seen by others as not respecting other people's time. This is because you might have only allotted a certain amount of time for this conversation, yet the other person has something different in mind. Practice ending what you want to say a few sentences shy of everything. Know when to stop!

Why should you always take notes?

Note taking is one of the simplest ways to be seen as a leader, and as someone engaged in the organization, that not enough people do. You can easily see those who are disengaged in the meeting. They stare off into space. They might even be doodling (which is much better than not having your pen in hand at all), but they clearly are not listening to what's going on. First, before you go into a meeting, make sure you get a glass of water or a cup of coffee. This way you start off alert. Next, sit as close to the meeting facilitator as possible so you catch as much of what they say as possible. Then make sure you have at least two pens in case one stops working, or you have one to lend to that one person who almost never has one.

Now you are ready to focus on the information and put it down on paper. Some of the best ideas I've had on solving a particular problem came to me while listening and taking notes during a meeting. I might even get the opportunity to share what I came up with during because I was listening the entire time and know the perfect place in which to interject my idea. Your notes are also an excellent place to refer back to in case of a disagreement or dispute, you will look much better and more put together when you are arguing your point from a notepad full of notes, while the other person simply has their hands.

The last point on note taking is that it shows another sign of respect to a person who may be able to help you in the future, besides its obvious practical benefits. The more you edify those around you, the more they are going to want to do the same for you. These are such simple cues yet we take them for granted. Let these help you, and continue growing your reputation today.

Why you should train yourself to never complain unless you have at least one solution.

Problems are absolutely everywhere. That's another problem, that there are so many of them going around! I've observed

over the years that one of the best, most passionate and ener-
getic discussions people have while at work, sometimes many
times per day, is around the problems of the day, and particularly at this same place of employment. At the same time what
I find most comical and disturbing is that 100% of the participants in these sessions have the power to fix everything they
are complaining about. This is when I made the commitment
to myself at that particular workplace, and to myself in life,
that I would never complain about something that was in my
power to control. This isn't what winners do. This is what vic-
tims and losers do.

Make the vow today that you will never complain about anything at work, or in a meeting without having thought through
at least one viable solution to bring up in response to this problem. Back to doing more than what is asked of you. You don't
have to do this, but it sure would help things at your job, and
even better set an example of how to do it and not just talk
about doing it. People who do this are also well on their way to
become indispensable at these same jobs. Just so you know, it's
these same indispensable people who never get laid off from
jobs, but instead get promoted because they just fired the other
old boss who did nothing but complain and never fixed anything. Meanwhile you were never asked to, yet you fixed a lot of
things. I know who I'd want around, what about you? Refocus
your efforts and energy into thinking of solutions for the problems of the day, not joining in when everyone else is just thinking about how to do less.

Why should you listen twice as much as you speak?

Listening more than you speak is actually one those habits
that millionaires live by. They are always good listeners and
go out of their way to listen to you. They don't like bragging
about anything they have or success they've attained, but they
are very generous usually when answering questions so long

as the right questions are asked. If not they are content and comfortable being quiet and listening. I say all of this to let you know that it is okay to be silent and enjoy this feeling. This is also definitely related to saying less, but this suggestion only takes it a step further by suggesting you actually try it out for a week and time yourself as you speak. In the beginning, and especially on the phone, it will seem as if you are not listening, when in reality you are simply letting the other person speak freely. It gets good when some people you're talking to won't even realize what's going on and they will literally talk until one of you has to abruptly end the conversation. And then when it does end, they probably won't notice. The amount of information you can glean from not speaking as much and listening more will astound you. You will learn more about the people around you and their intentions just because you are listening more. You might even find that instructions or other pieces of material that you listen to will make more sense.

As we said before, people love to hear themselves talk because deep down we all want to feel as if we have something to contribute to the world, which is true, but usually the things that people are qualified to speak on are rarely what they end up talking about. Once again you edify by just listening.

Why should you seek as much information about your position as possible?

Experts don't get fired or laid off, and are usually paid very well. Every professional athlete you see in the NBA, NFL, MLB or NHL are all experts in their particular sport. CEOs, inventors and scientists are all experts. Movie stars? They are experts too. How does one become an expert, and therefore the highest paid in their respective profession? You already know the answer because we've listed it about a dozen times so far in the book, but I'll say it once more in case you missed it: Practice. The cool thing is that we can become an expert at whatever we choose to, and we can literally start today. All we have to do is pick something that we really like. This makes getting good at it easy too. The problem is that most people hate their jobs so they never really get really good at it. Most people think if they hate it, why invest anymore time in it than what I have to. As a result they stay at the most basic levels at their job because of it. It's another creation riddle really. If you were better at your job, wouldn't you like it more? Or if you had more fun at work, wouldn't want to get even better at it? In other words if you don't like your job, quit. Then go and find something you really want to do so you can become an expert and resource at it. If not you will continue hating your job and being bad it just as easily.

🔍 Millionaire Mannerism:

If you hate your job, quit, and go find something to become an expert in.

Get a mentor at your job and inquire on how they got so good at whatever it is you do. I'm sure they will say they read everything they could about the subject, none of it was required, and they took risks on the path to becoming an expert. This is because until you go and try something new, how do you know how good you really are at something? Don't let fear or the expectations of others define you.

🔍 Millionaire Mannerism:

Don't let fear or the expectations of others define you.

Why should you respectfully challenge all assumptions?

My last suggestion in becoming a great colleague, boss, or expert in your workplace is to ask as many questions as possible about why something is to be done. This one step alone will separate you. You see many people ask why something needs to be done as a way to evaluate how much work they need to do. If this is your intention do not ask questions, because that intention will become evident very quickly, but rather ask questions because you genuinely want to understand the inner workings of the process. Ask questions because you want to know what your boss is thinking and how something could possibly be done better. I've heard it said that sometimes asking the right questions is better than always knowing the answers. Therefore it is critical to your advancement that you practice asking questions, and the right ones, and being quiet enough to hear the answer.

There are also folks who ask questions as a means to make other people look bad. This malicious and spiteful behavior might gain you a few fans and supporters in the short-term, but I assure you that these are the wrong types of fans, friends and supporters. The ones you want and need shun this type of behavior, and know that if you think in terms of showing someone up they probably don't want you on their team anyway. To ensure this is the case, make sure you have the right attitude. This is one of curiosity and not one of interrogation. Remember, you are not the police, so don't ask questions as if you were. When people sense they are being set up or backed into a corner, they do not respond well. Simply humble yourself and you're almost guaranteed to get good answers to your questions. Because keep in mind, your first win is to get the question asked, but the war's goal is to get the question answered!

⊙ Millionaire Mannerism:

Do not interrogate when asking questions, because when people sense they are being set up they do not respond well.

The other main reason for asking questions is for you to challenge what everyone else may have already accepted. Conventional wisdom is right a lot of the time but is sure as heck is wrong a lot too. Therefore take a risk and ask the question that everyone else is thinking. Meanwhile everyone gets an answer, and you look good for it.

Millionaire Morals:

- Always do more than what is asked.
- Listen twice as much as you speak.

Action:

1. Write out a list of questions you would like asked.
2. Present at least one solution during a meeting or unsolicited this week.
3. Quit if you hate your job! Then use chapters 1-11 to help you find a job you love.

CHAPTER 12
The Art of conversation.

How to be known as the best conversationalist around.

This is one of my favorite subjects to both speak on and write about, because it is something that both men and women, and the young and old can use, relate to, and get better from, and that is becoming a better conversationalist. Sensationalism is something that we hear a lot when it comes to over the top news reporting or antics by professional athletes. Truth be told, the word sensational can and should be used to refer to the range of topics you should be open to discussing during a conversation. All too often we stick to safe topics (which is not to be confused with non-controversial) and those that don't require much thought to engage in. The best conversation occurs when you are responding to stimulI from the environment in which you find yourself, or when you go in with a few choice questions you can ask anyone, anytime. I'll give you examples of both.

Some questions to always go into a setting with include:

1. What do you do for a living? And why did you choose that?
2. Do you have children? What are their names? How did you choose their names?

3. What are you most proud about your kids so far in their lives?
4. What do you like to do after work or in your spare time? How did you develop such a hobby?
5. What are you reading? How did you hear about that book?
6. What was the last really funny joke you heard?

The examples are literally endless, but these are a couple of the questions I try my best to ask as many people as I can. They are designed around getting people to speak and engage with you, not talk at you. They are also designed to force active listening because the answers you receive will not be cookie cutter in nature. This is because no one, in whatever setting you find yourself, ever asks these type of questions. Dare to be different, then dare to be interested in this stranger and smile the entire time. You will be called a brilliant conversationalist in no time.

Ask questions about things that interest other people. Hint, first find out what other people are interested in!

Another sure-fire way to be able to ask great questions of those in attendance at a particular function is to find out beforehand what attendees will likely be interested in. If you're going to a fundraiser for an art gallery, you might want to ask attendees who their favorite artists are, and of course add in the almighty "why" after every answer as a follow-up, and to dig beyond the first surface-y response. Another quick way to open the door to a great conversation is to observe. Observe the details and similarities of the people you come in contact with and ask them about whatever you see. An example of this might be that if you notice everyone in a room has on the same lapel pin indicating membership in an organization, ask them about the organization, or how they became affiliated with it. This helps your cause even more because whatever organization they may describe may be something you might be interested in, so you're actually winning twice here!

All the methods of becoming a great conversationalist start with asking questions, being interested in their answers, and ultimately being interested in other people. This is why meeting new people is such an exciting thing, because you never know what information or hidden connections you can uncover by simply chatting with strangers. You could find out you're actually not strangers with this person at all, or find out you're in the presence of someone really important, all by asking the right questions and being really interested in what the other person has to say.

This is also yet another instance of making someone else feel important. Many times during our days we are cut off or not allowed to fully express ourselves. This is why therapists are some of the highest paid people in the country. You pay them to simply listen. Although I'm not saying to just listen and not say anything, as soon as you are quiet long enough to let someone else express a complete thought, you will probably become a memorable person to them because we are not afforded this luxury often, sadly not even by our own significant others or spouses sometimes. Listening is key, and listening with empathy is even better.

How to tell awesome stories.

Excitement and emotion are your best allies in story telling during any setting. Entire books have been written on the subject so this is really just an overview. First you have to control your voice, pitch and tone enough to get the attention of those around you to indicate you have something to say. You then have approximately 10 to 15 seconds to tell a cool enough introduction that people actually want to hear the rest of it. The story you tell should have a beginning, middle and end just like any other, but don't be too long and drawn out on any one detail. Your story should also most definitely have lots of elements of humor so you keep the attention of your audience. A few jokes only aid in the build up toward the conclusion, punch line or end of the story.

Make sure you gauge your audience as to the appropriateness of your story beforehand. If it's a too little risqué you might want to tone down certain details, especially if the host is somewhat of a prude. This is another reason to hold back a bit or change it up between different pieces. However if it's your event, let it rip. This also means you probably have a bit more leeway in terms of ramping up to your joke's middle and end. But again, make sure you have some humorous elements included along the way.

⊕ Millionaire Mannerism:

The way you do one thing is the way you do all things. So do them all excellently.

Lastly, great stories are always mostly true. You don't want to be the guy at the party telling someone else's story or exaggerating so much you might as well have just made the whole story up to begin with. This is also bad for you in case someone is present who may have heard you tell this story before. Now they're hearing you tell a completely different version? That probably doesn't bode well for your established reputation, even in a social setting. People can and will take the smallest things as an indication of your larger character, and rightly so. As the old saying goes, "as you do one thing, is the way you do all things." Show respect and humility, but have some fun, even when storytelling.

Tell awesome stories but don't be this guy.

Here's a quick truth about showmanship and social settings. No one likes a showboat. You will be the smoothest and most sophisticated person in many of the rooms you enter after reading this book. The point is to make it look effortless, fluid, and unrehearsed when you do it. The lunk, douchebag, ham, lush or one-upper as we call them is anything but. This is the guy who wears too much cologne, who's laughing too hard at his own jokes, and trying to one-up everyone in attendance by telling a bigger, better, and grander story. He exaggerates too much, most of his "facts" are taken from other people's stories, and he usually has no one around to corroborate any of what he's saying. Pretty convenient don't you think? This person is not very popular once he turns his back. My solemn and humble advice is to make sure you don't become this guy.

This is also the guy who has no concept of outside voice, inside voice or party voice. He only has one volume setting; loud. Another characteristic of this type of guy is that he is very stingy with his compliments to your face, but secretly loves what you have on. He then takes to Google to find out where he can get one of whatever it is he likes and very well might order it on the spot. When this happens, do like I do and just tell him "Oh this, I got it in New York." Man, the looks I get with this little trick. For them, just working up the nerve to ask where you got it from is compliment enough coming from this type. So don't reveal the brand, the store, or any identifying marks until he musters up a real compliment!

My advice to avoid falling into this type of behavior is to make sure you are paying close attention to the body language of the folks around you. If you see them losing interest in what you are talking about, draw them back in with a question. If you see their eyes travelling someplace else, travel with them. Whatever you do, don't talk too much.

One question that will immediately set you apart.

The uncommon and remarkable thing, or the "purple cow" as marketing guru Seth Godin refers to it, is the thing that is much easier to remember. It is the thing or occurrence you're almost forced to remember because it was so different from anything or everything you've seen. Your goal during social interactions is to be this for those you're interacting with. How can you do this? Why should you do this? Eventually you'll come to discover that most of the time you want to be selling something, and that you represent you and your brand at all times. So therefore the more memorable you are on a day-to-day and interaction-to-interaction basis, the easier you will establish your brand identity (another way of saying reputation). We've covered it briefly already, but one of the best questions you can ask of anyone, anywhere is the question why?

"Why" makes people think of why they think a certain thing. It puts people on the spot and forces them to clarify their positions on certain things. It elicits excitement from most people because they usually never get to explain the "whys" behind certain things they do, say or think. Why allows people to reveal their deepest and hidden strategies. These are the type of things people long to share but have no outlet through which to do so. Once you are able to become that outlet for even a small number of people, you instantly become remarkable, exciting, and most importantly, memorable. You think you'll have an easier time getting in front of the person you make feel this important when it comes time to sell something? Probably not. Lastly, just observe the glimmer in the person's eye as you speak to them about something they love to do. It will literally bring a smile to your face every time you see it happen. It's almost like magic, which is part of your reward too. The better you make people feel, the better you make yourself feel, which then becomes part of the self-fulfilling prophecy of how these concepts can improve whole areas of our individual lives and those we come in contact with every day. As they say, it then becomes easier to become the change we want to see in others.

Why should you talk about things that arouse passion in you?

The cool thing about being the one who is asking the questions is that you will more times than not (I hope) have thought of a great answer to your own question. This means when you go to ask a question about the current war, or who the most interesting person is currently to this person, you already have your own passionate answer ready to go. When the topic comes back around to you, you then get a chance to showcase how powerful and interesting you are by answering your own question. Passion allows us to become exponentially more interesting because our own glimmer comes through. Yes, the same glimmer we are attempting to bring out of others is the same one we are constantly looking to bring out of ourselves. As we've talked about before as well, the better you are at something, the better you want to be at the same thing, and then the better you work at it and the better you become. It becomes a self-fulfilling prophecy of success and winning that was all orchestrated because you focused on what you liked, instead of what you didn't like. This takes some time to really grasp but it starts with asking yourself, what am I really good at? What do I really like doing? Those answers will start you on a journey to becoming your best self. Then you will look up and these same principles will aid you along your journey.

🔘 Millionaire Mannerism:

When you bring out another person's glimmer, you bring out your own.

Back to conversing. Speaking passionately about topics that interest you is the best way to never appear dry, boring or dull. Einstein might have been the worst conversationalist ever when talking about cooking or babies, but I guarantee if you got him going about math or physics you probably couldn't shut him up, because the glimmer would have had him by then.

Show respect for other's opinions.

As we move on, we've talked much about what to do, but will now switch directions just a bit toward things that you probably don't want to do as much of. And by not as much, let me clarify, I mean never! There are three magical words that when you use them in nearly any setting you are guaranteeing yourself at least a slight battle, maybe even one that will last a bit beyond whatever setting you're in. Those words are "you are wrong." For the record, it doesn't matter if the person is right or wrong. Most of the time, you'd be right in observing the incorrectness of this person's statement, but what you just did was awaken something in them as old as the human language itself; their defense mechanism. Now you have forced them to defend themselves with all their might, no matter how wrong they are, and how right you are. You have now forced them to spitefully look for every flaw in every one of your arguments because now you have made them look bad, uneducated, ignorant, or all of these, and they're going to make you pay.

Instead, of disagreeing with someone in such an adversarial manner, just say "that's an interesting opinion," and then simply and calmly state yours. One thing I've learned is that in normal conversations away from the Internet and TV, everyone becomes an expert, or just saw or read some report that solidifies their expertise. Therefore any of these "experts" in front of you will so vehemently defend their position that you would think it's themselves in the news story. This is the negative power associated with telling someone they're wrong. The worst thing that can happen is that you tell someone they're wrong and they turn out to be a one-upper! Now you have a situation on your hands because they are going to literally shout you and your facts down all the way and have everyone thinking you were actually the wrong, misguided, and ignorant one. Now how's that for being right? When anger and ego is in play, very little else will make sense, so do your best to steer clear of this potent mix.

Why should you never interrupt?

This section could've easily been included with the one-upper or talk of ego. This is because whenever you cut someone off, especially to interject your own point, you make people angry. They will think you are rude, and they will be right. We just talked about the defense of right and wrong. There really is no such thing in a social setting, and where there is no fact-checker present. Our objective in this book is to arm you with the necessary tools to be a Millionaire Manners Ambassador, not a person who's right all the time. I know a lot of miserable broke people who are right an awful lot of the time. The problem is this becomes their quest instead of winning. I had a colleague once who because he had no college degree was always in a battle of wits with our boss. In the end the boss won and my colleague ended up leaving the company (at my boss's request) because he was tired of debating every little detail whenever he gave an instruction, whereas this colleague just wanted to show everyone how smart he was despite not having a degree.

Don't let your internal battle slow down your potential results in the real world. Your reputation and how you conduct yourself and showcase your manners are far more important and far more valuable than being right or getting your words in edgewise. Again, practice listening and responding, not waiting for your turn to speak.

🔍 Millionaire Mannerism:

There's a big difference in listening, and waiting for your turn to speak.

Beware of TMI.

Couth is the egg when baking a cake. It's savvy interpersonal connecting. It's taking all the cues and putting them together. It's knowing when you have a general rapport going or the person you're talking to isn't really interested. It's also one of the key ingredients to know you have already or are about to share too much information (TMI)! TMI isn't insurmountable by any means, but it can lead to a few awkward moments as folks around you formulate normal responses to whatever inappropriate tidbit you might've shared. Things about your home life shouldn't be shared. Embarrassing stories about your boss or coworkers should probably be left out. Letting people know how gassy you are after the Mexican food you ate can be kept to yourself too. The examples are way too numerous to attempt to put them all here, so I'll suggest another empathy exercise here. When was the last time you said to yourself, "Gee, I sure wish I didn't know this about so-and-so." This is probably a really good example of what not to share.

Ultimately TMI comes down to your own personal level of shame and embarrassment meter. There are some people who have an extremely high confidence level and an ego so big it takes quite a lot for them to become embarrassed, while there are some of us who hardly want to share anything for fear of being labeled an over-sharer. Somewhere in the middle is the right answer though. Just think before you share!

Four things to never say during your conversation.

We'll end the chapter with a collection of four things and phrases you should never say when chatting or conversing with strangers, or anyone else for that matter.

"Am I boring you?" Let me just say this, if you have to ask, then the answer is yes. If you feel this happening to you, or Lord forbid you are on a date or a more private social setting, quickly reach in your bag of questions, and lead with this "So, can I ask you a question?" Then lay it out! This is one of my favorite tricks for reengaging a lost person or audience. The curiosity of what you might ask them will overwhelm them almost every time, to the point it exceeds the potential of them being asked something embarrassing or something that won't have them looking their best. But never ask if you're boring them.

"Huh? What? Say what?" Or anything else rude. Substitute these annoying "I didn't hear" fillers for more appropriate ones like "pardon me," "excuse me," or "would you mind repeating that? I couldn't make you out all the way." I despise when my kids use these and I despise it even more when grown people use them, especially when addressing me. I usually will repeat one back to them and they will catch themselves. Try that. Another quick way to avoid this altogether is to, once you initiate conversation, ask the person right away to increase their volume so you don't have to ask after they're 50 or 100 words in and now have to repeat their whole story again!

"Stop me if I've told you this story before." Here's a quick way to kill a mood. If the story is good, just tell it again, don't get everyone's permission. I've told some stories that are so good people will ask me to tell it again, versus no that one sucked. Chances are there will be some new people around anyway so they get to enjoy it brand new.

Correcting someone's grammar. This is right up there with blatantly telling them they are wrong or cutting them off when speaking. Who are you, their tenth-grade English teacher? Even your teacher wasn't rude about it. She'd just mark your paper to hell a couple times and you'd get the picture. As painful as it is, people will just think this person is nervous, but their attention and annoyance will quickly turn to you once you become Mr. Know-It-All grammar guy. You'll probably be seen as smug or a jerk. If you really want to help this person, get them a copy of this book or have them email me!

Millionaire Morals:

- Asking questions and listening is the foundation for being a great conversationalist.
- Make sure to always show respect for other's opinions; dislike and respect can co-exist.
- Beware of sharing TMI!

Action:

1. Commit the sample questions to memory or your own version.
2. Commit the four "Never Say Me" phrases to memory, then never say them!

CHAPTER 13

When to wear what?

Wardrobe essentials.

Having a wardrobe that is as awesome as your attitude is not as much of a stretch as you might think. Simplicity is what you want to start with in terms of putting together pieces and looks that will suit you both now and in the future (pun intended). There are several wardrobe essentials and special skills that the Millionaire Manners Ambassador prides himself on knowing and any gentleman in general would be remiss without mastering.

The first thing you want to nail down is what colors look good on you, and what colors don't. The more knowledge of self you have (and you thought this was just in reference to your skill set), the better equipped you will be in dressing yourself well and in the way that best portrays you. Favorite colors don't apply to suits per se, but they do to accessories like ties, shirts and shoes. Color can be either a huge aid in your strategy or a big distraction as you interact with other people.

The main point of this chapter and the topics we will discuss is to ensure that as you are putting excellent information inside your brain, you are equally as flattering when presenting yourself in all aspects. No one wants an awesome gift inside a box with shredded and torn up wrapping paper. There is no anticipation this way. The opposite is true as well and we see this every day, where someone who has no substance and has just jumped ahead to a chapter like this gets all the accolades but can't truly compete. Let's master the icing.

Why are clothes important?

Demeanor and attitude go hand in hand and they can make or break you. When we control our thoughts and protect our mental state as if our lives depended on it is usually when we fare the best, in multiple situations. Doesn't it make sense to add as many things to our toolkit as possible that aid in making our attitude and demeanor bulletproof from negativity? Absolutely! This is the practical purpose that dressing your best serves. Besides the other wonderful side effects of having people compliment you, people wanting to know where you shop, and lots of attention from the opposite sex, your clothing choices have a direct impact on how you see yourself.

Here's a quick litmus test. How would you feel about going to a board meeting today in a sweat suit? It's just a sweat suit, and it's just a meeting, right? Let's say you're the CEO; you're still the boss right? Of course not! Chances are that you'd feel like a slob and out of place. This is why certain places have a non-negotiable dress code. Places like a court room, a dinner club or any respectable after-hours spot has a bare minimum of style decorum you must abide by if you expect entry.

Lastly, clothes can do magic in terms of helping you "big" yourself up, sort of like that good old puffer fish we spoke about chapters back. When you don't feel like you belong, or that you might not be fully prepared to handle a particular situation, I promise you that if you are the best dressed person there, all these self-doubts and negative speech you're giving yourself will evaporate into thin air. You can do this just by putting on those special clothes. Whatever you reserve for those special occasions, consider wearing this type of stuff more often, because isn't preparing to win and impress daily a special occasion?

One suit.

Classic is one of those words people throw around all the time with no true understanding . People talk about classic musical albums, classic cars, and definitely classic movies. Most commonly, people talk classics is in the area of style and fashion. We'll get into this discussion more later on in the chapter, but classic is more about style than fashion. Let me explain: Fashion will say this is the new designer who's making this particular item, whereas classic style will dictate that the essence of this particular item will never change and never die. That, in a nutshell, is where classic comes into play, style and fashion wise. Who decides what is classic is an entirely different conversation. But what I would like to do is quickly define one staple in a man's wardrobe that is so classic it has been around for over one hundred years. You can wear this look to any of the places I listed in the last section, or even take off one piece of it, and wear it almost anywhere. What I'm referring to you is your classic blue, pinstriped power suit.

Its nickname is the power suit because that's how often people of power wear it. Ironically though, never has an item also been worn so much by those who aspire to power as well, as is the case with the blue pinstriped power suit. When you pair this with a colorful tie, say red, light blue, pink or yellow, the message this look sends is that not only have you arrived, you are also in charge.

If you do not own one of these, I'd suggest going out and buying one right away. As a general, rule when buying a suit try your best to stay away from places where there is no one working in the suit department. You want to buy from a store who has a staff of people who are knowledgeable about fit and style, and can recommend alterations if necessary.

Seasonal/Occasion.

Seasons are a really tough thing to plan for, and just as tough to dress for. Therefore, I encourage all our readers to exercise some common sense when dressing, especially as the seasons are changing. Having lived on the East Coast for the majority of my life, I can tell you that our weather patterns range from skipping some seasons altogether (we miss you spring), to a schizophrenic like mixture of sixty degree days in winter and snow mid-spring. All of this is to say, do yourself a favor and wait a few weeks in to a particular season before you completely disregard the seasonal looks of the previous one. Case in point, as soon as March hits, every year I can count on some jerk breaking out his white pants about sixty days too soon. Just because the calendar says March, or even that spring has officially arrived, is no reason to catch a cold or think because you wear a t-shirt and no jacket on a fifty degree day that you actually have control over the weather. It does not work this way, and all you will do is again, catch a cold, or look silly when it comes time to attend an outing.

So we've covered wearing white too early. The same goes for wearing "springy" pastels. Take a moment, check the calendar, and make the call as to whether or not your attire will be appropriate for wherever you are going.

What watch to where.

Watches are one of the areas where you can say a lot without ever opening your mouth. My recommendation is to go for slim watches almost every time. They are understated and elegant, and don't need to shout in order to catch someone's eye. There are three types of watches, if you were going to own just three, that I think are an excellent addition to any collection, and that you can wear with a variety of outfits in a variety of settings.

The first one is my favorite, and that is a solid stainless-steel watch. They can range in price from $99 to a couple hundred dollars but almost always catch looks because they are shiny and on the larger size. These types of watches have their roots in both the nautical arena as well as aviation so their function was just as important as their form. A nice stainless-steel watch goes well with any suit no matter black or brown shoes. Just make sure you always go for a neutral watch face color.

My next choice is the brown leather banded watch. Again, this watch will go well with "Casualty Friday" and your nice pair of creased khakis, and is also great with your jeans and brown loafers after-hours. Leather band watches can also be dressed up nicely. If you want to splurge a bit, then go for the brown and black leather so you can switch it up from the stainless-steel.

My last choice and suggestion is that you get one really good, really cool looking digital watch. This is one you can wear with any outfit to give you that sporty look, but of course it's ideal for weekend outdoor chores or for when you hit the gym. There are more innovative designs coming out in the digital arena so shop around and get one that will spark up a nice conversation too.

If you have to ask this, you already know the answer.

A critical area for us to define before we go any further is the difference between seeking approval and asking for an opinion. A pretty clear indicator would be do you give options when seeking an opinion, or do you ask a vague open ended question about a particular topic, or worse yet your outfit? If you're not being specific with your questions, the chances are you are really seeking approval, and you need to stop quickly. That is the definition you should have fixed firmly in your mind, and with it, make sure you never ask this approval seeking question: "How does this look?"

Women ask this question a lot, because unlike us men, they usually make a decision pretty quickly as to what they dislike. If a woman is asking you this question, what she is really waiting for is a compliment. She just wanted a clever way to draw your attention to what she was wearing, but she knew she looked good. The rule of thumb for this question for men however is this: If you need to ask, you already have the answer. Instead, practice giving two or more options when you come up to a decision about your outfit. Ask your friend or significant other, but keep your question specific. If not you will frustrate yourself and the poor person who you asked this question, because as hard as they try to answer the question, they'll never give you the one you're looking for. Go with your gut. Sometimes self-policing is the best kind, especially if you've read information like this. It's all stored right there for you to access, you just can't be afraid to do it.

Why should you keep your shoes looking good at all times?

Detail oriented people are almost always in leadership positions and in the proper position to make things happen. Does what I'm about to compare this to make it the case? Probably not, but it will absolutely increase your chances of looking the part on your way to making this characteristic possible and a permanent addition to your personality. What I'm talking about is keeping your shoes spotless whenever you go out. I know women and other people who are in positions of power and the first place they look on a person is their shoes. Of course, it's possible to be a jerk or worse and have on clean shoes, but that's not our concern because I'm sure none of our readers are thinking like that. What I am saying is that a couple of simple things and a bit of effort can ensure you do not end up in the dirty shoe box.

Before you even think of cleaning your shoes, you have to make sure you own a pair worth investing the time necessary to even want to clean them. As is the case with almost all the lessons we've been talking about, most don't cost a thing. Shoes do, and how much you decide to pay for them is a personal choice. Many people believe you won't be blessed with more until you truly appreciate and care for all that you have currently. I agree with this 100% and it even applies to shoes. If you paid under $100 it really doesn't matter because if you're next to a guy with a wrinkled suit and expensive muddy shoes that he purchased just because someone told him to, I'd pick our Millionaire Manners Ambassador every single time, and most everyone else would too.

Tips for Loving your Shoes. (And, in turn, having them love you.)

- Clean/Wipe them down after each wear. I don't care if we're talking sneakers or wingtips, start the habit of cleaning your shoes afterwards each time you wear them. This way crust or dirt won't set in and make it harder to clean next time. Not doing this instantly ages your shoes.
- Never wear the same pair of shoes (if you can help it) two days in a row. And certainly don't wear them three days in row! This is a simple tip that has allowed me to maintain some shoes in my collection for over ten years. Simple wear and tear takes years off your shoe's life, so letting them catch a breather is not a bad thing. And no, just because you know you're not wearing them tomorrow is not an excuse to not clean them after you take them off!
- Find your neighborhood cobbler today! If you don't know what a cobbler is, let's start there. A cobbler is a shoemaker by training, but one who is an expert at repairing, mending and maintaining your shoe's life and wellbeing. Think of it as taking your shoes to the spa (yes, men should most certainly go to the spa for manicures and pedicures). Your cobbler can repair tears, replace heels, and most importantly shine and protect your shoes to the point of looking

almost new. This is an invaluable service. Now you don't have to wait until you're randomly in the airport before you can enjoy a good shoe shine.

- Invest in a couple pairs of solid cedar wood shoe trees. These are to be used for your more special pairs. They not only provide a nice smell for your shoes, but they also absorb any moisture that may be left in the shoe from the day's wear; and if you can't find shoe trees, or don't want to spend the money for a couple pairs, use socks to stuff the toes and body of the shoe and tie them up. Socks can be just as useful in helping the shoe keep its shape and eliminate moisture which leads to odor causing bacteria.
- Invest in a shoe horn. One of my pet peeves are folks who walk/mash on the back of their shoes simply because they might be a little too snug to put on because they don't use a shoe horn! This small piece of metal or plastic will save your thumbs and back of your shoe. Walking on the back of your shoes is not good and shortens the shoe's life.

Style versus fashion.

Personal choice and style is so deeply at the root of what we teach in Millionaire Manners, that how you choose to represent yourself when there is no right way becomes the fun part. This is never more evident than when we talk fashion versus style. The quickest and simplest way to define this argument is really as fashion being **what** you wear, and style being **how** you wear it. With this simple definition you begin to see that it really doesn't matter what labels or brands you wear, but rather if it looks good, and more importantly, feels good, then it is good for you. Many times we see and hear of people talking about this designer or that designer but have no personal style established so they just jump from brand to brand. This is the definition of a label whore. Someone who just follows trends and fads but has no real identity beyond this.

Don't get me wrong, there are several brands that I check for quite regularly, but there is no one brand I buy exclusively, or to which I entirely subscribe as if everything bearing one particular label is good. But again, this is a personal choice. My recommendation is to make sure you have thought about the types of things you like in your wardrobe, not only about what brands you think are popular or tend to gravitate. This is also directly related to the conversation about which pieces of fashion or style are classic versus those that are merely fads.

The beauty of it all is that nothing is permanent and you can make the decision tomorrow to change your style completely. People do this every single day in fact. What you don't want to do is develop a reputation (there it is again) as someone who does what is popular or easy. Above all else, make sure you are personally happy with the style choices you make, because without this happiness present, nothing else will compliment you. Lastly, make a pact about this as you've made about other aspects of your life since beginning the journey in this book, to resolve to never be afraid to take a risk when it comes to your style or fashion choices. This is the only way to discover things and grow.

Why is fit so important?

Custom is the 2000s answer to being a member of the new "Cult of Individuality" where anything from cell phone cases, to sneakers, to cars and motorcycles can be made into your personal one of a kind creation. Why should your clothing feel any less fancy than any of these other things that won't pay you back half as nice as a well-fitting shirt? Proper fit gives you the appearance of having spent much more on whatever it is you're wearing. This is why movies, TV shows, and people on the red carpet always look good, because they have personal stylists and other people who are paid to make sure their clothes fit them perfectly. This is precisely why I don't recommend buying a suit or any other important piece of clothing from a store that does not have a salesperson on staff to help you find your perfect fit.

This step will make your entire outfit look way more expensive, and hopefully make your attitude better and more confident to match. Think of all those pictures of clothing in the 80s and 90s, everything people wore during those times was huge! Now with so many brands making lines of menswear for a variety of body types, i.e. athletic, trim, slim and others, it makes it that much easier for you to find and purchase the perfect fit from your favorite store. But first you need to come to the realization that you probably are used to buying your clothing too big. Therefore the next time you shop, buy approximately one size down, or at least try it on. How good it feels might surprise you, and open a whole new world to you.

What is the one question you should always ask and what's the one thing you should always do?

Dress code, as we've spoken about, is the bare minimum for every event. Try your best to never simply abide by the dress code. The minimum rules are in place for those who are concerned with being average, in my humble opinion. To test this theory, have you ever seen rules about overdressing for an event? Of course not. Gentlemen and Millionaire Manners Ambassadors alike don't have to worry about things like this because we are striving to be maximum oriented individuals in all that we do. But, one small question can save you from being dressed wrong.

Before you leave for the day, no matter if it's for work, school, or an event, always ask what the weather will be like! This may seem like common sense, but how many people do you know buy umbrellas every time it rains? I know a few myself. Ask any street vendor when they sell the most umbrellas and I will bet any amount of money that it's never *before* it rains, but rather *after* the rain has started. If there's one thing I hate, it's being stuck outside in a favorite pair of suede loafers just because I was in too much of a rush to simply see if rain, snow or any other weather event was in the forecast. You always want to be prepared and dressed appropriately so simply incorporate this into your style routine.

This one small tip can save you a ton of time, money on dry-cleaning, and from having to buy new suede shoes.

Quick tips on dressing well.

Terms like "dressed well" and the like are completely opinion based, as we've covered. Down to the color of your socks, how much cologne you apply, how you respond, and so on and so forth are very much personal choices. I've laid out many guidelines to help you narrow your choices and ultimately make the best decision for you, but here's another list of items that when applied together, or with other info in this book, give you a much higher shot at coming out on top, no matter what your "top" is.

Here they are:

1. Your belt should match your shoes nine out of ten times. This is one of the first basics of dressing well that I learned. A conscientious man always has on a belt the same shade as his shoes. Once again, it's about an attention to detail and taking pride in your appearance that many men simply don't value. This is precisely why you will run circles around them in the game of life.

2. Learn how to tie a tie at least two different ways. I take back what I said previously about my first lesson in dressing well. My first most basic lesson was how to tie a tie. I was so proud when I finally figured it out and couldn't stop demonstrating it for my father. I actually think he wanted to strangle me with that tie. He was so happy he gave me one of his ties. The other cool thing that happened was I then figured out there was more

than one way to tie one. Talk about a light bulb! Do yourself a favor and learn the Windsor & double Windsor knots ASAP!

3. Don't over apply cologne. If there's a scent that you have to smell on yourself more than the scent of respectability, then spray on. Your personal scent should be faint, not overpowering. The cool thing is that when you have a couple different scented personal care products, plus your cologne, plus your own chemistry that if you do it properly you will have a scent all your own and completely unique to you. The one thing you don't want is for people to know you're coming before you've entered the room!

4. Never wear athletic socks anywhere except to the gym. This is one of my personal rules that I simply do not break and a pet peeve of mine that makes me shudder when I see it. I really enjoy the various styles of socks that are available to us men in new and exciting colors, besides just good old black and white, which are still perfect for the gym, but you will never catch me destroying a good outfit with something as crazy as thick black or white gym socks. Instead, get creative and try to see on how many levels you can bring out the favorite aspects of your outfit. Let them out, don't hold them back!

Millionaire Morals:

- Style and fashion aren't the same; find your own style and worry about fashion later.
- Strive to avoid dressing to dress codes.
- Dressing to the details shows a lot about you.

Action:

1. Get a blue suit; if you already own one, make sure it fits!
2. Remember the quick tips to dressing well.

CHAPTER 14

Traffic is no reason to lose your cool. Traffic manners and car etiquette.

One simple way to eliminate road rage forever.

Millionaire Manners is all about learning to control your emotions, your attitude, and to assist you in making sense in a sometimes insensible world. Our objective is not to attempt to control those around us, but through our own actions make things considerably more predictable. When you find yourself behind the wheel, this is no different than any of the other scenarios we have talked about in detail. The first tip I am going to give you in relation to controlling your road rage is that you control your own time.

I have identified this as the number one cause of stress inducing road rage simply because we lose control from being late. All you have to do is plan on leaving simply 15-20 minutes earlier than you normally would, and half the issue is gone. People tend to revert back to their lower selves when confronted with choices that cause them direct harm. Hence, if I am late, I don't have time to miss the next light, let alone let you over because you missed your turn. My civility goes out the window because if I'm late, I could miss my meeting, be reprimanded by my boss, or worse. The Millionaire Manners Ambassador is in full control of this situation by controlling his time. We don't have to let our manners take a back seat, because we are never late. Embrace the power that comes from being early everywhere you go. You immediately put people on the defensive, improve your posture, and let people know you are a serious individual, all just by being on time. It will also significantly reduce your stress when driving.

The root of all road rage.

Ego can be a life saver or a life destroyer if we don't prove to ourselves that we are the boss. It can be the little voice telling you to apologize first, or the same voice telling you that you're well within your rights to never speak to your brother, sister or childhood friend again because they called you fat or told you they didn't like your outfit. Ego can make us do silly things if we let it run us unchecked. I begin with this brief description because road rage, and all other rage directed at others for that matter, has its roots right here. We get upset when we drive because we think another person has slighted us, and therefore hurt our ego. Ego is defined as simply our own self-esteem. However, the more common definition is the one we allow to get us in all sorts of trouble, and that is "an inflated opinion or view of ourselves." This is by no means a knock on a healthy ego, one that goes hand in hand with our new found confidence, but rather an unhealthy view of ourselves which says "I'm the most important person on this road, or in this room." The thing is though this very well may be the case, the strong man does not belittle others in order to make himself feel bigger. If you and everyone else already know how big you are, there's no real need to go out of your way to show and tell everyone.

Other drivers do not know you, and they aren't really thinking of you at all. In case you didn't know this, now you do, and that officially makes you the "bigger" person. You have just been blessed with this consciousness, and must now use it in as many situations as possible. This means forgiving those who transgress you because they don't have the same understanding, self-image and confidence as you. They're just trying to satisfy their needs right now and you happen to be on your way. I recommend practicing your breathing while driving and focusing on becoming one with your surroundings. As you breathe you will become less conscious of your actual driving experience, and therefore much less pervious to stress. Leave early and breathe, and you'll be smiling more behind the wheel before you know it.

Another simple way to avoid road rage.

Besides controlling your time and making the pact to leave your house early enough to arrive everywhere at least 15 minutes early, there is one more simple tip to help alleviate any controllable stress from the road. The tip is that if you are going someplace either unfamiliar or that you haven't been before, do yourself a favor and look up and at least glance at some basic directions before you leave. This one step alone will ease your mind, save time, and maybe even save you from an accident. A huge percentage of traffic accidents today are caused by texting, emailing, using social media while we drive, or by attempting to follow GPS directions. Not knowing where you are going will have you skipping lanes in traffic, cutting people off, driving too slow, or taking off slowly from green lights. The funny thing is that I just listed about four items off this chapter's don't do list.

Another cool thing about knowing where you are going is that now you get to play the occasional Good Samaritan who, when stopped and asked for directions can now offer help. What a great feeling! All in all it's about being in control at all times, and letting nothing distract you from your focus or objective once you arrive wherever you are headed. We've all heard and read about information being power, and even more powerful is applied knowledge. Here's your chance to put those smartphones to work and make you smarter for a change!

How to immediately feel better after someone upsets you in traffic.

What do the words Granny, Grammy, Grandma and Nana all have in common? For starters they usually represent the terms of endearment and nicknames for the only woman on the planet that is more respected, loved and cherished than our own mothers, and that is our mother's mother, aka our grand-mother. One simple trick that I've come to utilize in both driving situations, as well as many others is to simply imagine that the fool who just cut me off, gave me the finger, or switched lanes a little too close to my bumper without using his turn signals is none other than my own grandmother. I'm happy to share this little trick with you because you've probably read about or heard about some things to help you with your anger behind the wheel and maybe some of them worked, and maybe they didn't. It's my aim to give you as many original tactics and strategies as possible with the hope that at least one of them works for you. This is a trick I will almost guarantee.

Our grandmothers are usually sweet old ladies who mean nothing but to see us do our best. They are concerned when they see us frowning or upset, and they always feed us when we see them. So picturing this little old lady in her finest attire staring at us with those eyes is just what we need to cool us down as we are about to shoot flames from our ears we're so upset with what another driver just did. Instead of overreacting just picture Grandma. If this doesn't work, then picture she's sitting right next to you instead. I've found that this actually works better than just picturing her in the other car. This is because it's easy to get upset and keep driving, as we may not even make eye contact with the person who offended us, but if Granny is sitting right there there's no escaping her gaze. So think of your Grandma and keep your cool!

One of the last and most basic tenets of Millionaire Manners has always been to simply ask for whatever it is you desire. Ironically, we probably even learned this once or twice from our Grammies. Why we have forgotten this valuable lesson just because we get behind a steering wheel I have no idea, but if you would like to get over simply ask.

The top driving do not's!

1. **Nudging pedestrians along with your horn**. This is a quick way to embarrass yourself if you happen to be driving with company or even a young lady. People want to see how you behave with strangers. Is it with care and delicacy, or are you harsh and in a rush? Blowing your horn at pedestrians is a quick way to tell people that not only are you not in control of your emotions (because this group of strangers walking just upset you that much), you are a pretty rude person too. Again, this can be seen as you thinking your time is more valuable than the next person's simply because you are driving and they are walking. Don't be a presumptuous jerk, or even a regular jerk. Don't use your horn unnecessarily. Save it for emergencies, and be a gentleman.

2. **Playing your music too loud**. Only immature folks have a deep desire to be seen all the time. It's different for you to look awesome when you are seen, but to draw unnecessary attention isn't always the best thing. As someone who enjoys music played loudly sometimes, this is for me, not for everyone around me. If you feel like your music is disturbing someone else, simply lower it. Besides if you have subwoofers or an extra amp, yet it sounds like your car is about to be ripped apart, they

probably can't hear the actual music anyway. Pay the extra money for insulation, or just turn it down.

3. **Driving too slowly**. This is the one instance where tailgating is probably warranted. There are some people, again myself included, that just enjoy the thrill of fast driving for time to time. No excuse if your need for speed is self-induced. See the first section of this chapter for clarification. However, it is just plain rude to drive at or below the posted speed limit then drive anywhere besides the far right lane. I've even seen police pull people over for doing this, and accidents caused simply because folks were driving too slowly. Get off the expressway if you don't like driving fast, or just move with the flow of traffic, but keep it moving!

4. **Double parking**. I've seen death threats thrown at the perpetrators of this egregious and borderline human rights violation. It defies logic how someone can think that either (a) they can predict exactly when the person who they've blocked in will come out from concluding their business, or (b) that their time is more important than the next person's. Either way I tend to slightly agree with at least the threat portion of the death threat.

5. **Driving with your high beams on, permanently**. I've seen people do this for a number of reasons, and even done one or two of them myself, but to disregard other drivers on the road by doing this is the height of disrespect and incivility that we are striving so hard to end. I live in an area that is heavily populated by deer and they wreak havoc at nightfall. This means during drives in the woods where there are twists and turns everywhere, the high beam is critical. It takes effort, but you should turn them on and off when you see oncoming traffic. How did you like it the last time you were blinded? If you

figured out the fact that your high beams will still work even when one of your normal headlamps is out, don't do it! Just go and get your headlight replaced. You can usually even do it yourself. Whatever you do, make sure you're not of those guys who feel the need to install those extra-bright aftermarket headlights. They are unnecessary and obnoxious.

6. **Honking at traffic lights when they turn green**. The half a second ago that the light turned green is so insignificant that in this amount of time, you probably can't even complete a thought, let alone get any significant amount closer to your destination. Give it just a moment before you blow this person in front of you away with your horn. Perhaps they got distracted, as we all do, or maybe they're like me and purposely wait at least a half-second *after* the light turns green to ensure no one is about to smash into me. If the person ahead of you doesn't go after the count of one-one thousand, two-one thousand, then lightly double tap your horn as a non-aggressive reminder.

7. **Tailgating**. Let me quickly take back what I said. My typing rage has subsided. There is never a good time to tailgate someone. Not only do you significantly decrease your cushion to react in the event of an accident, it's also rude. The quickest, easiest and most painless way to deal with the person who needs to be tailgated is to go around. If you are being tailgated, switch lanes and continue with your leisurely drive. And by the way, please take more leisurely drives. You probably need them. We all do.

8. **Not cleaning the top of your car off during winter**. If you live in an area that gets a decent amount of snow then you know exactly what I'm talking about. This is a

real hazard. These huge sheets of snow and ice can hit bystanders, and it's also terribly inefficient to drive more than 30mph with a huge amount of snow/ice on your roof. It's dangerous for others and your car looks ridiculous. Take the extra three minutes and clean the top of your car. We all thank you!

9. **Not using turn signals.** This might seem like a small one in comparison to the other items on this list, but it's definitely not. There's nothing worse than waiting five minutes to make a turn, only to find out you could've gone ten minutes earlier but the jerk in front of you wasn't actually turning! Or the person who thinks it's normal to jet across several lanes to exit the highway, all without signaling. Just click it, even if it's for a second. It lets everyone know you're coming through, and maybe even that you've arrived.

10. **Not letting other cars merge over.** It's not their fault the lane is ending, and the driver next to you probably doesn't work for your state's highway administration. Therefore just let them over. However if it is one of those folks who deliberately drives the shoulder to skip ahead of all the other waiting cars, I don't have that much sympathy. They knew what they were doing.

The moral of the story is to continue to model exactly what it is you wish to see from those around you. Anytime you are a passenger or have someone riding with you, it's a great time to model your philosophies and explain them to others. Take advantage!

Millionaire Morals:

- Road rage is ungentlemanly and shows a lack of control.
- Road rage, and all rage, has its roots in unchecked ego.

Action:

1. Read, then reread, the Don'ts and pledge against them!
2. Leave 15+ minutes early for EVERY appointment, no matter how informal; use the informal events to practice the habit for the big ones. Then walk in like you own the place.
3. Always picture Granny riding shotgun.

Introducing T.H.E.T.O.P.H.A.T. system for forming Millionaire Manners daily.

We've covered a ton of information so far, and I hope you don't feel overwhelmed. If you do feel this is unlike anything that you've ever heard, that is actually a good thing. You should be getting that tingly feeling like you can sense something big is happening to you. This is the tide of the changing seasons, and the signs of you becoming better, stronger, higher-powered, and iron-willed. However, in order to make sure you always have something to refer back to, I've created a quick system for helping you remember. It's called T.H.E.T.O.P.H.A.T. system for forming Millionaire Manners daily.

By remembering T.H.E.T.O.P.H.A.T. and the funny picture it paints, you will be able to recall all the most powerful lessons we've covered in this book. Before I describe the system to you, think of the picture of a top hat. Where have you seen it? What does it automatically make you think of? Hopefully it makes you think of a certain regalness, a clean and proper setting, a fancy place, and more. The top hat was worn during the 1910s through 1930s and represented all these things and more. They were worn by aristocrats, businessmen, and those of a higher class. While the top hat is no longer as popular today as it once was, it still represents these things. My favorite piece in Monopoly is, you guessed it, the top hat!

Think first impressions

One of our very first lessons remains part of the foundation of everything we're establishing, and that is to ensure you are always considering your first impression on anyone you meet. We know you only have one chance to meet someone for the first time. It can be either good or bad, the choice is yours. It's not the end of the world, but it sure helps everything else you're looking to achieve by getting in the stance of trustworthy, competent and gentlemanly as soon as possible.

Handshake and eye contact

Two extremely important topics that we discussed early on. These two are key in establishing great posture, and the stern handshake goes a long way in ridding your initial meeting of any intimidation. Surprisingly enough, those who would intimidate often back off, or tone down their intention to intimidate on this aspect alone. Make sure that these two go hand in hand, eye contact and the firm handshake that is. And again, if you suffer from Essential Palmar Hyperhidrosis, aka sweaty palms, no problem, just keep a handkerchief handy and dry them off before making contact. This requires a bit of planning, but then again so does winning at the game of life. No one is successful overnight without significant planning and preparation. The cool thing is to just not look like it.

Extra mile

Need I say more? This concept alone has spawned entire volumes written on it. It encompasses everything from doing more than is required of you at your job to changing your entire mindset from minimums to maximums, which for many people is tough to do. Not because it is actually tough, but because most people don't know why they should do anything extra in life. No one has explained that the most successful people in history first gave away their best products and services, then charged for them. They demonstrated why they should be promoted from their current job, not tell the boss they plan on doing more once they are promoted. Life doesn't work that way, and those that pride themselves on doing enough just to get by will ultimately just get by. Apply the concept of doing more to every aspect of your life, including in how you deal with people and everything will change. There is nothing written anywhere that says you must hold open a door, or help that old lady at the grocery store with her bags. You do those things because they help people and help you form the habit of doing so. Extra is a choice, a lifestyle, one that will always pay you back.

The introduction

Always being prepared to introduce yourself and give a couple of fun facts is something that can be useful in a number of situations. As you put your newfound Millionaire Manner skills to the test, you'll be introducing yourself quite a bit. There are tons of events to do this at; networking, work clubs, social clubs, and for our students, after school clubs. The more comfortable you are talking about yourself, the easier it will be for others to do the same. Even in getting feedback.

Open your mouth to smile first and speak first!

One of the other chief rules and foundational habits needed to succeed in this material is the concept of being the first mover, aka taking initiative. The Millionaire Manners Ambassador doesn't wait to be spoken to or for someone else to introduce themselves, if we want to meet someone, we simply walk up to them, smile and give them the introduction you've been practicing. Immediately the other person is going to consider you somebody. You weren't intimidated because they were the keynote speaker (this time) and not you. This is a practiced art, like many of the skills here, and you will learn it.

Posture and body language

Posture is the blank canvas that your actions and attitude get painted on. If it's busted, then everything else will be busted too. You have to master the art of shoulders back, chest out, and chin up. Try it any time you're feeling down about anything, and almost instantly you will feel the life re-enter your body. This is because you just subconsciously told the world and everyone in it, especially those who can see you coming, that you are in charge. They had to either give you exactly what you came for, or get out of your way. This is one of the best feelings there is.

Happy thoughts

When you are down, remember your own personal Dandelion List. These are the things that make you smile, even when you're having a day from hell. These things will help you get a smile on your face that will slowly bring it all back around. This is like a smile jumpstarter! Then when you are back to feeling down again, just try your best to always keep happy thoughts in there. These are the thoughts that will translate into your actions, and your actions will turn into results. Of course our results are how we keep score against whatever it is we want to do in life. As you can see, thoughts are an extremely big deal.

Ask open ended questions

The key to the great conversationalist is to ask questions. But remember, not just any questions, but open-ended questions about the other person. If you can listen twice as much as you speak, it was a great conversation for the other person, and it should have been for you too. Never forget that because you have this info, it's on you to use it. I know you want to talk about yourself and prove to everyone around how interesting you are, but by the time you make everyone around you feel like a million bucks, you will be off counting yours, and they will have questions for you!

Twelve x twelve x twelve

One of my favorites. How do you look from 12 feet away, how do you look and smell from 12 inches, and what are the first 12 words out of your mouth? If you can answer all these questions and still have a smile on your face, then you're on the right track. But if you see people pack up when they see you coming, and/or they're not immediately intrigued as to who you are, then you are probably doing something wrong and need to consult with this book again, or your honest feedback partner, spouse, significant other, or whomever. Keep those mints everywhere, a small bottle of smell good and even a toothbrush at your desk. You never know when you might get called to an impromptu meeting with the President. Challenge yourself to be better than you ever thought you could be.

Again, T.H.E.T.O.P.H.A.T. formula is there for you to have top of mind (just like the hat) whenever you get into tough situations. Breathe, think of what letter suits you and do what you know you should. Not what's easy, not what will merely get you through the situation, but rather what will make you shine. Do what will paint you as remarkable and buy you time to prove that you truly are. That's what T.H.E.T.O.P.H.A.T. is for, and winners are who it is for!

Millionaire Morals:

- Practice, practice, practice.

Action:

1. Practice, practice, practice!

CHAPTER 16

Why women absolutely love gentlemen, but hate chumps.

Psychologically speaking, all women want a man like their dad.

In psychosexual developmental psychology, Sigmund Freud, through his research on the subject, came to the conclusion that there is a strong correlation between the feelings and connection we have with the opposite sex parent, and how we manifest those feelings later in life. This is why the he came to coin the term "Oedipus complex," which denotes the son's desire not for his actual mother, but for a woman who strongly resembles his mother, physically and in character. The reverse of this phenomena is known at the "Electra complex," where females have the same connection and desire to be with a man who strongly reminds them of their fathers. This is not always a negative thing. Especially if their father is a strong personality who has instilled a great pride in his daughter, her wanting her man to at least share some of these same morals, values and ethics she has grown accustomed to seeing is in fact a positive thing. This is where our manners training comes into play.

Knowing that so much of what we teach is based on getting to know the other person, and genuinely looking to build long lasting and meaningful rapport, you can see why this is so valuable. Going out of your way to learn about your potential partner's father is a very worthwhile investment, as you can learn much about what makes your lady tick! Why she prefers you behave in a certain way, and how exactly it's best for you to cater to this, just as likewise it would be beneficial for her to learn these same things about you from spending time with your mother.

Ultimately though, women want someone who instills in them the greatest of all daddy traits, and that is the feeling of security. This is not just from a physical standpoint. As a man, will you be emotionally stable for your woman? Will you be her protector, maintainer, and if necessary her teacher? These are the roles that the first man in her life played, and that is what she will look to you for. Make sure you are prepared by doing the proper research, and keep studying your Millionaire Manners Manual!

Why do women love confident men?

Women of all ages, shapes and sizes want many of the same things, and usually in unison. One of the first on that that list is your ability to defend them in almost any situation. This means attacks on their character, their physical person, and anything in between. The confident man knows and understands that in order for him to defend someone else, he has to have confidence in himself that he has the skills, talents, abilities and flat-out backbone to defend his woman when necessary. To bring it back to the father notion, this is something else that fathers always do for their daughters. Therefore it has to be present in the psyche and toolkit of any man who wishes to hold down their woman in a moment of strife.

This same confidence must also translate into his ability to maintain for and provide the things his woman needs. These range from the physical and emotional, to the material and financial. All of them take supreme confidence in order to pull off. We've discussed in a number of places throughout the book that everything we see before us today began as a vibrational thought in someone's mind. Through concentration and activity those thoughts became things, and it started because the thinker had confidence it would eventually happen. This is one of the best ways to formalize a plan, but first it starts with the picture in your head of what's possible.

Why the attempt is many times better than the result.

Here is where originality takes a front seat to simply following a blueprint that you've seen used a ton of times. Originality is your ability to take pieces of things that are old and make something entirely new from them. This is also where confidence rears its head once again as your tool of choice, as many women enjoy being given or shown a fresh approach to a standard problem for men: How do we get their attention without breaking the law. Also for most women, it's the thought that counts even more than the actual execution of whatever harebrained scheme you might have in store for them.

When courting, try something new. We haven't gone into full-on rules for dating but so much of it hinges on your comfort level with taking some risks and not reading from the same manual as everyone else. You can get ideas just from channeling how your new outlook and mannerisms make you feel. You can't do the same old things after you decide to hold the door open for your lady every time, or open her car door. You can't have a great conversation at a local club, which is the same place you're more likely to run into someone who you don't want to see, so you better try a new locale, and so on. Try some new things, and the results will amaze you. But of course, you must first rid your old self of fear.

What is a chump?

Chumps and pushovers are the exact opposite of what we're building here with Millionaire Manners. Because we're talking about the opposite sex in this section, let's talk about what it means to be a chump. I must warn you that I am speaking purely from an anecdotal perspective because I have zero experience in the chump field, but I have seen a few operate in my day so I'm pretty good at seeing them coming. It's somewhat simple to spot them too. They agree with pretty much everything coming out of everyone's mouth. This includes their woman. They enthusiastically laugh at all of the boss's jokes, especially the ones that aren't all that funny. He also mumbles a lot when you ask him a question first and he hasn't heard anyone else answer before him, so shame on you for asking, because he simply hasn't had time to put his thoughts together. Another unmistakable characteristic is that he will not only go along with everyone, but he does this to not rock the boat, say anything memorable, or form an original thought for fear it will put him further on the hook for original thought.

He is usually scared of his own shadow and even more afraid of being the target of anger from his woman, if he can get one, so he hides. He avoids confrontation because he has not read anything on the subject matter or trained himself to confidently handle when someone challenges him, his work or his thoughts. My hope is that you have been given some of the many tools that will equip you to handle confrontation, and the wisdom to never start one. Women, employers and decision makers do not wish to keep chumps, pushovers or yes men around . When they want your opinion they will give it to you. My only reason in bridging this topic is to ensure whatever of these particular characteristics you might still have a small remnant of, you rid yourself of, and that you are able to help identify them in people closest you that you may help them. Mostly importantly though, make sure you know that women do not find this attractive.

Why is being polite not being a chump?

All throughout this journey you are sure to encounter a certain contingent of individuals who see all this "manners stuff" as soft, wimpy, or not useful to their lives. This is the opposite of the case, and those who feel this way are those who need it most. In mastering one's self, you are privy to a side of yourself no one will get a chance to see, only that they see your results. The internal battle that wages on is yours and yours alone. This is precisely why you will reap the benefits of this battle. To control one's primal reactions to situations when a harsher response may be warranted is true self-control. Smiling when someone is attempting to get the better of you is actually the most control you can have, because meanwhile this person is smiling at you, you are smiling right back, because to respond in a negative way is to lose control and complete the transfer of power. As Millionaire Manners Ambassadors we simply listen, observe, and file away real and/or perceived slights because they are secondary to our actual goal.

It is often said that the last battlefield is the mind, and the ultimate prize is your attention/consciousness. It is this reason and this reason alone why we need to practice these skills now more than ever before. It is this battle of self that has the ultimate in feel good rewards too, and that is the ability to walk away. This is a skill and a weapon that some people never master, and therefore never realize how powerful they are. Combine this with a "you have everything to gain" attitude and nothing will stop you. Remember, if you can't control yourself, how can you expect to be trusted with the responsibility of a woman?

🏵 Millionaire Mannerism:

Take what you want; if it is too much you will be corrected.

Why you should always speak to a girl's father if you want to marry her: A brief lesson in old world chivalry.

In the old times, which can even still be seen in manly movies like The Godfather, the man who desired a woman had two courtships he had to plan out and master, but it's not in the order you're thinking. I know it sounds weird, but the first courtship was from the man to father of the woman, then the woman herself. If you did not get past the father, then you did not pass go, did not get $200 and most certainly didn't get the big prize. Fast forward to today and this once customary act has all but gone extinct. I challenge you to help revive this old-world custom, with only a few slight updates necessary. I recommend that before you get too serious, and once your intentions are known, that it is you who broaches the subject of meeting her father before she even gets a chance to. This shows two things. First it shows, that unlike the chump we spoke about earlier, you are not afraid of a good old fashioned (positive) confrontation. The second thing it shows is that, despite you likely being more scared of this than anything you've had to do, especially if you really like her, you are supremely confident in yourself and have a backbone. Keep in mind the proactive "take initiative approach" can be and should be applied to many scenarios in life. The more headfirst you can make things, the less time you give yourself to think yourself right out of doing, and immediately ensuring you lose. We haven't mentioned one of my favorite quotes, but now is a great time to: "Fortune favors the bold." So be bold and take what you want. If it is too much you will be corrected.

🅶 Millionaire Mannerism:

Fortune favors the bold, so feel fortunate, never forget favors and be bold.

Millionaire Morals:

- The Oedipus and Electra complexes can be valuable tools.
- Attempts are a great way to practice everything.

Action:

1. Plan time with your spouse or significant other's mother or father.

EPILOGUE:

What are your responsibilities and expectations after reading this book?

Use this secret formula, or nothing in this book will work for you!

Before we end with my final thoughts and parting words of encouragement, as this is sort of like a graduation, there is a combination of ingredients that are so potent, that by themselves any one will bring you much success in life. We've discussed each one in detail, but never specifically with each other and in this form. What I am about to give you, please read, re-read, and read again for without this recipe, your Millionaire Manners will only half work. The magical formula is:

One Part Genuineness

One Part Humility

One Part Confidence

One Part Empathy

Genuiness x Humility x Confidence x Empathy =
Millionaire Manners Ambassador

Everything else is a cheap imitation and carbon copy. Genuineness will allow all your messages to get through, even if your delivery is a little rougher than we'd like. If your emotion has you on edge, genuineness will still allow you to be seen in love.

Humility is the emotional volume control that ensures you approach the person and situation in general with the proper perspective. Ultimately we are warriors for right and we lead by example. Humility allows you to do this by downplaying your own importance in the situation. You ask for little yet give much in return. You are concerned with results and not being harsh. Harshness is remembered for the wrong reasons, yet humility is love and is received as such.

As your confidence level grows this is the power where you must to stay the course and believe what you are doing and saying is going to impact those around you. It is knowing before you start that you are going to win. It is bringing people with you because you have earned their trust and now will help them produce. Confidence is knowing you have value and not being nervous, or at least too nervous, to prove it.

Lastly, empathy is you going beyond the step of seeing yourself in the other person's shoes. You assume their thoughts, feelings, fears, likes and dislikes. You then even see yourself through the eyes of the other person. How else would you know or even care if you have wronged this person. This is the first step in making sure you offend as few people as possible on the road to your goals.

Giving and accepting compliments.

Keep in mind that we are all human and subject to prejudices, stereotypes and excessive media brainwashing. Having these disclaimers in the back of your mind at all times will ensure you don't kill yourself every time something doesn't work for you. Just try it again. As we apply this formula to all situations make sure you remember the basics when accepting and giving compliments. This may seem like a strange place to reiterate what seems like such a basic topic, but you'd be surprised at (a) the number of people who get this simple thing wrong, and (b) how it illustrates all of our four ingredients perfectly.

In order to give a compliment the first thing it must be is genuine. That's right, it doesn't even have to be true, but if you mean it, then magically it just became true to the recipient. Compliments are in and of themselves humble in nature because you are paying homage to the person you are complimenting and giving your approval of something they have done or said. It also takes an extreme amount of confidence to compliment, because it shows you are not so caught up in yourself that you can't acknowledge when someone else is doing their thing too. This is a big person, and as you select the right words to say you ensure you do not give the infamous "non-compliment." You guessed it, this takes empathy. Saying something like "You're smaller than in your picture," is not the same as saying, "You look great!" See the difference?

So in not applying the formula to compliments, hopefully you see the obvious dilemma. When you choose to apply it, you'll be a wizard. The last reminder is for accepting compliments. **Be gracious**, and do not negate their compliment (since now you know what actually goes into someone mustering up the strength to give one) by turning around and giving them a fake, disingenuous, unthoughtful non-compliment just because your own confidence level was too low to accept it. And here's one last hint: If you think someone is trying to make fun of you or give a disingenuous compliment, just give a big "thank you!" and keep moving. They'll look like the silly one.

The quickest way to genuineness.

How do you master genuineness? Here's a quick tip I love to recommend. I must say that it can get a little awkward if you don't have a great imagination, but practice it and you'll be fine.

The tip is to picture everyone with whom you need to muster great genuineness with as the woman of your dreams. Think of her as you speak to the next person you meet, and watch the change. Please know though that there is a huge difference in flirting and speaking with genuineness, but it also starts with just telling the truth. If you believe what you say (and not in a George Constanza from Seinfeld type way), then it should be evident in your speech. This fact alone will allow for a certain amount of genuineness to always be there, but the rest that you may need takes practice. Again, as a rule of thumb you should always use the following litmus test before you say anything: Is it kind, is it true, and is it necessary? This alone will probably have you cut half your words anyway!

Millionaire Mannerism:

Think before you speak: Is it true, kind and necessary?

Keeping the morality in the marrow of manners (Styleand Substance).

It is very easy, as I've said before, for shysters and cons to get ahold of this book and become a proverbial treasure trove of new and improved techniques and use them to dupe unsuspecting people. I know this fact because I have studied these principles for years and know they work. But that would make you a con-artist, and me in turn complicit with your con game. I will not be a part of anyone's con game. Therefore to avoid this from happening and to ensure I can sleep well at night, I offer the sincerest of explanations of Millionaire Manners.

These teachings are not meant to simply "put lipstick on a pig," but rather help you transform your way of thinking about people and how you interact with them. I don't want to dress up a box of poo in a pretty little bow and then send you on your way. No, I want to help facilitate real change so you're not just another jerk pretending to be polite until he gets the girl, the job, or the short-term answer you're looking for.

I don't want jerks, I want an army of men who are serious about their manners, etiquette, and their morals. See, morals are the marrow of manners. Say that three times fast with me. Morals are the marrow of morals, meaning they are the substance to the style of your speech, they are the flavor of the meat and the actual gift inside the pretty box. We spoke about your own personal code early in the book, yet here it is once again. It is time to put the two together as you embark on this journey. You will not last for the long haul if you are missing either one, and the sad part is that no amount of reading can teach the marrow either. You have to look for it inside yourself. The formula will work and assist you in this, but you must give it value, then show everyone why you do it.

What are your personal expectations for reading this book?

As you conclude the reading of this manual, ask yourself, what are my goals after reading this material? More money at my job? Better grades? More recognition, more dates and more love from the ladies? More confidence at social events? Any of these are worthy, but first you must choose something to which you will apply some of what you learned. Not every situation will afford you the opportunity to practice everything in this book, but as you keep your eyes open, many chances occur every day. But you must be paying attention, and looking with the intention to win. Along with this is simply proving to yourself that you can be better then what you've been, and that there are immediate rewards for doing so. But it all begins with the decision.

One of my favorite mini-anecdotes is as follows:

At a particular town sat a gatekeeper. This gatekeeper's job was to welcome all the travelers and visitors to the town and answer their questions. He was a solemn greeter, but pleasant nonetheless. On a particular day the gatekeeper saw two travelers that arrived separately to the town yet asked of him the same question. This was unusual for the gatekeeper so he asked a question of his own. As the first traveler arrived to the town he asked what type of townspeople lived there. The gatekeeper responded with this question: "How were the people where you came from?" The traveler answered that they were all extremely polite, warm and welcoming. They all treated him as if he were family, the traveler said. The gatekeeper replied that the traveler would find the people in his town the exact same. The traveler thanked the gatekeeper, marveled at his good luck and entered the town whistling.

The second traveler that day arrived with a very different look on his face, one of apprehension, fear and worry. He hurriedly asked the gatekeeper, "What type of people reside in this town?" The gatekeeper asked, "Well, how were they where you came from?" The traveler proceeded to tell the gatekeeper about all the dishonest people he met, how everyone was trying to steal from him, and no one even bothered to greet him or give him any directions. He had a miserable time. The gatekeeper politely replied to the traveler's question that he would, unfortunately, find this town's people exactly the same. The traveler didn't thank the gatekeeper but rather brushed by him, cursed his bad luck and mumbled as he entered.

The moral: Both travelers came from the same town.

Share this information with everyone you know but make sure you use the formula. That is if you are actually interested in helping them change. Genuiness x Humility x Confidence x Empathy is a potent mixture so please apply it as you model these principles and as you tell people about them on a day-to-day basis. Communicate with care, with love and with good intentions and you can change everything.